LUCKNOW IMPRINTS

A Poetic and Historical Account of
the Golden City of the East

SANOBAR HAIDER
SHWETA MISHRA "shawryaa"

INDIA · SINGAPORE · MALAYSIA

Notion Press Media Pvt Ltd

No. 50, Chettiyar Agaram Main Road,
Vanagaram, Chennai, Tamil Nadu – 600 095

First Published by Notion Press 2021

ISBN 979-8-88503-613-9

Contents

Author's Note

LOVE YOU LUCKNOW...

By: Sanobar Haider

The idea of writing something about Lucknow always floated in my sub conscious mind. Being a history student the love for digging into the past has never ceased to excite me. Living in the city ever since my birth, being educated, employed and married in this fabled city gives me the reason enough to pen down my thoughts and express my love for my birth place. I have grown up breathing Lucknow and... I speak Lucknow, the style of addressing aap-janab making me easily identifiable as a Lucknowite. I can well express my feelings in the lines of the famous poet Josh Malihabadi *"कल भी जिसके तसकीरे थे, अंजुमन-दर-अंजुमन, दास्तान-दर-दास्तान, शाम-ए-अवध है आज भी";* I am proud to be a part of the most sophisticated and celebrated cultures of the Indian subcontinent.

However, the importance of growing up in a city such as Lucknow does not dawn upon you in the beginning. The glitz and glamour of the bigger cities casting a shadow over the slow and eased out life in Lucknow.

But now, driving through the Rumi Darwaza, the main ceremonial gate leading to the Bara Imambara, one is awed not just by the beauty of its perfectly proportioned arches, towering minarets and elegant pillars but also the sense of history that breathes through its ancient walls. The magnificence of the architecture is humbling. The walks are soothing and the poetic feel of the city is enthralling. Lucknow is like a piece of poetry written on the fabric of Indian History, having all the characteristics of a culture in itself. From the surma for the eyes to the huqqas for the soul to the modern day glint in the sun there is something for everyone. It appears apparently that Lucknow has lost most of its original charm in this new frenetic race for development, However, I still believe that, despite the changes, 'there's no place quite like Lucknow'

The idea of writing a book snow balled into pen and paper with my colleague and dear friend Shweta Mishra. Both of us desired to create something different in a style not often used by writers of History and English literature. The blend of history and literature dates back to times immemorial and definitely promises to offer a captivating platter to the readers. History in the conventional sense can be defined as a record of real events that happened in the past while literature occupies a special place in transforming and supporting the emotions of people.

And so we began our sojourn on a topic close to our hearts. Then came the corona crisis and the unexpected lockdown which gave us time to stay at home with family. This stay at home period was utilized to complete and finalise our work, amidst the global pandemic. With the family members staying together and gradually working out a routine for the day, I with the moral support of my ever so ready to help husband went ahead to finalise our book.

Through this write up I would like to express my gratefulness to my family for bearing with me during my secluded periods on my laptop. My husband Mr. SM Haider Rizvi for his constant support, guidance and mentoring, my boys for attending my errands and letting me take hours away from their time table, my mom and mom in law and sisters for unconditional love, and last but not the least to our students for being an enthusiastic lot in all our endeavours.

– ***Sanobar Haider***

Author's Note

LUCKNOW AUR HUM...

By: Shweta Mishra "shawryaa"

कभी कलम ने रुख मोड़ लिया
कभी सियाही ने दम तोड़ दिया
इस पल यहाँ उस पल वहाँ
अल्फ़ाज़ों को ढूंढते ख्यालों ने
मनमाना बर्ताव खूब किया।

That's how the journey has been. Writing this book has been a roller coaster ride when several memories turned live and the speed of their appearances was faster than I could record...

Memories are memories due to their pastness and things bygone are clear pictures in still waters. Their abstraction lends them that element of pain, and the haziness of this past lies just an arm span away...across that mirror lies my childhood, one arm span more and one more mirror and this present will be on the other end too...hazy yet clear... in me yet out.

Even today I can feel my past as much alive as ever, just as it was when I was seven. Under that neem tree I had my haven. A platform raised around the neem tree covered one-third of the height of the trunk. I remember the barks that I could pull out from the broad stem; those black, brown and hollow barks with red ants that moved in a disciplined line...I remember that for many hours it was just that tree and me. I remember that I could never have enough of the trunk. Right and left and round and round I played around that tree. Nothing was important as in those moments it was only the tree that was my sole concern. With chalks and wood charcoal I made birds and peacocks on the plinth. Madhumati with its red and pink flowers that I collected basket full, gulmohar with its crimson ones decorated the side road just in front of our house and covered the road half red and the flowers of harsingaar that my sister and I collected to make bracelets and necklaces... that's the fragrance of childhood Lucknow.

The smell of stove when *ghee*, carrot and flour were cooked for hours, that smell lingers still. Blankets, groundnuts and *chai* to beat the wintry chill; *thanda paani*, *shikanji* and *sharbat* for sweltering summer thrill; *lassi* and shakes of all kinds topped with thick layered cream, dry fruits and ice... Lucknow is a city that has always been too ethnic with desi vibes.

The book is my tribute to the beloved city. Since childhood the city has nurtured me in its caring lap and with the gradual passage of time the experience of being a part of this extravagant city dawned like the morning sun and blossomed like a lovely flower. Lucknow is an experience that grows steadily and then lasts perpetually.

Lucknow has matured in me from being just a location on the envelopes, from being just a part of my address, from being just a word that is inanimate and dimensionless, to become my identity, my roots, an experience that is vibrant with life and colors, to being a comrade and an intimate part of my soul.

मुझे इश्क अश्क से है या अश्क को इश्क मुझसे
इस फितूर में रही तो कहीं मंजिल मिल भी जाएगी
पर लखनऊ में पड़े तेरे कदम और लखनऊ में रहे मेरे कदम
इनके निशान न समेटी तो तय है कि मंजिल खो ही जाएगी

Lucknow in evening *gupshups*

Lucknow in corner *wali paan* shops

Lucknow in unending *khwaish*

Lucknow in irrepressible *kashish*

Lucknow in cultured *zarra nawazi*

Lucknow in fond *tabiyat nasaazi*

Lucknow in oomph *ada*

Lucknow in tender *khata*

Lucknow in velvety *zubaan*

Lucknow in courteous *shaan*

Lucknow in unremitting *intezaar*

Lucknow in *nazakat beshumaar*

Lucknow in craving *chahat*

Lucknow in silent *hasrat*

Lucknow in passionate *mohabbat*

Lucknow in ardent *ibadat*.

I offer my gratefulness to my dearest parents Shri G.N. Misra and Smt. Beena Misra, for their limitless love, for letting me experience their zeal through my work, for being my guiding light and for their huge support and motivation. I wish to thank the Almighty for lending me that unfailing spirit that was needed to complete this work. I thank Dr. Sanobar Haider for being a wonderful partner during this journey. I thank everyone in my life, and I thank this city for helping me make this book possible.

– *Shweta Mishra "shawryaa"*

Endnotes

gupshups: gossips

khwaish: yearning

kashish: temptation

zarra nawazi: due regard

tabiyat nasaazi: unwell

ada: grace

khata: mistake

zubaan: language

shaan: pride

intezaar: wait

nazakat beshumaar: elegance in abundance

chahat: wish/love

hasrat: desire

mohabbat: love

ibadat: worship

Foreword

Lucknow is a lifestyle city associated with Indo Persian architecture combined with a potpourri of European influences, and the intangibles of the politesse of pehley aap, Urdu Ghazals, Kathak, miniature paintings, its own gharana of music, its unique dumpukht and variegated cuisine, mangoes, kite flying, chikan and myriad handicrafts and the legendary tawaifs who came to be romanticized by Bollywood. The fabulously wealthy city flowered in the late Mughal period, was associated with the Nawabs, and was the eye of the storm in the great maelstrom of 1857. The British reconquered the city in alliance with the Sikhs and the Gurkhas, and systematically sacked the city and looted and demolished iconic structures like the Machi Bhawan and later the great Kaiserbagh palaces, in whose outhouses they settled the erstwhile Talukdars of Awadh. The fabled jewels, precious metals, paintings, arms, brocades and libraries were systematically plundered and found their way both into great European collections as well as the loot of soldiers. The British Residency came to symbolize the idea of Empire for the British.

Post 1858 witnessed the rise of the cow protection movements in U.P., the Urdu Devanagari conflict, Kisan movements and the freedom struggles and the gradual erosion of British hegemony culminating in Partition and Independence. Chattar Manzil and Farhat Baksh kothis which had housed the Nawabs and the Begums and subsequently the United

Services Club of the British, were symbolically handed over to the temple of the new India, the Central Drug Research Institute. Lucknow grew spatially as well as in numbers, and the inward migration from different parts of the state has changed both the social fabric and even the spoken tongue of the city.

The average citizen of Lucknow however still prides himself on his tehzeeb and tameez, a relatively languid lifestyle, a cosmopolitan outlook and a refinement of language, food festivals and fun which are intrinsically woven together. Lucknow also had a long tradition of rekhtis, which characterized the colloquial prose and poetry of women. I am happy that Dr. Sanobar Haider and Dr. Shweta Mishra seek to continue this tradition, through a jugalbandi form, sometimes between Urdu and English or sometimes just as a conversation to distil the memories of this city. Thank you for the mulaqat.

– ***Ravindra Singh***
Mr. Ravindra Singh IAS (Retd.)
Chairman,
India Literacy Board,
Former Secretary, Ministry of Culture,
Government of India

Lucknow – Ek Mulaqaat

Shweta:

कुछ तो बात है लखनऊ शहर की जो महसूस होती है साँसों से आँखों से
ये एक ऐसा तजुर्बा है जो तबीयत और मिज़ाज पर कुछ खुशनुमा असर करता है

Sanobar: Wow, what a lovely way to build a wondrous world of words before we embark upon a soulful journey into our beloved city of Lucknow...

Shweta: Hmm...The Ghats of Benaras reveal thousand stories at a time, and so do the Sangam and Kumbh of Allahabad. The Taj Mahal of Agra speaks aloud a love story. The state of Uttar Pradesh is dotted with towns, villages and cities that have a past to share. With evidence of how these places have come of age and evolved, we trace their history; and with ideas about their bygone days, we write their stories. Yet, we remain clueless about how these places have breathed and lived and loved in different corners, walls and hearts.

The capital of Uttar Pradesh, Lucknow, is just another city like every other. But like every other city, Lucknow is also different.

To trace that difference depends on every individual's perception of that city. My feel of Lucknow is my own perception of this land. Lucknow for me is unique, riveting and spectacular.

The birds of Lucknow...they are as calming as we are... equally gentle and dreamy.

Here dreams float somewhat more than in any other town... dreams in every eye...

Lucknow in whole, half and quarters...Lucknow in and around... Lucknow within...

To peep in Lucknow is to peep inside the hearts of the people here.

The verandahs and the courtyards in Lucknow are the ones where Lucknow sits

The air that surrounds Lucknow envelopes us with some strange ancient warmth.

Those who live in Lucknow can sense this antiquity.

It is exclusive and singular.

There are some images, some reveries in the eyes of the aged people of Lucknow. These images seem to sail like vessels in the deep sea, wanting to reach the silent shores that are carved and strewn at the same time. One would not know whether to gather all the scattered bits and pieces or to sway away with them to lie somewhere, unknown yet desirous...

That's what Lucknow has always been. It has layers and layers and layers to it. You would not want to unfold it as it looks more beautiful the more layered it is, the more wrapped it is, with beauty that increases each time you drape it and fuse it with embroidery.

Somehow, these embroidered sheets raise the fragile beauty of Lucknow and like an enchanted lover, all the people of Lucknow—in their own way, knowingly or unknowingly—woo their beloved city.

Sanobar: In the words of Asrarul Haq "Majaz" Lucknawi

इक नौ-बहार-ए नाज़ को ताके है फिर निगाह
वो नौ-बहार-ए नाज़ कि है जान-ए लखनऊ - मजाज़

The Ganga and Jamuna, two of the great rivers of India, meet and flow as one to the sea, together yet distinct.

The cosmopolitanism of modern Lucknow has its roots in the era of the Nawabs who ruled the Kingdom of Awadh in the 18th and 19th centuries. Awadh, comprising what is today the central region of Uttar Pradesh, was established in 1722 under Nawab Saadat Ali Khan. Having been a province of the waning Mughal empire since the mid-16th century, the fertile region, with its thriving agricultural economy, became one of the most prosperous regions in northern India. In 1775, the Nawabs established their capital at Lucknow. Soon, Lucknow became a cultural hub of art, architecture, learning and music under the patronage of the Nawabs, who had a refined sense for art in all its forms. The story is long and I shall indulge in its details.

Lucknow is a historic city, located on the banks of the river Gomti. Gomti is a tributary of the Ganga river and is believed to be the daughter of Rishi Vashishtha in Hindu mythology. Besides being religiously important, the river holds within its heart many stories of the past.

Traditionally, Lucknow was the capital of Awadh and was administered by the Nawabs during Mughal rule. In 1857, after the first war of Independence, the kingdom of Awadh passed into the control of the British empire.

Attempts by the British to change the identity of the kingdom failed despite the exile of Wajid Ali Shah, the erstwhile ruler. The musical traditions and the dance forms continue to make their presence felt on the cultural fabric of India even to this date.

Besides being known as the 'city of Nawabs', Lucknow has also been called the 'Constantinople of India', the 'Golden City of the East' and 'Shiraz-i-Hind' by historians and writers over the centuries.

This city has still kept its old-world charm intact, which is an appealing feature for tourists. It is no exaggeration to call the capital of Uttar Pradesh one of the finest cities of the country in terms of mannerisms and culture.

Shweta: Lucknow—when you breathe in and breathe out, the intervening space is Lucknow. The calm that sits on brows and then flies to perch on the heart, only to beat to its own rhythm, that calm is Lucknow.

Lucknow is an experience that is never enough. Like to have loved and lost; something you would want for your whole life yet know that it would not stay.

If I ask you what it is that makes you feel warm, which gives you happiness without any attached feeling of guilt; what is it that is sweet and cozy and protective as a mother's lap; what is it that nests your desires and harbours your optimism? Is it your home? Where we stay and prepare for our future; where we rest our energies and prepare to face the world; that is what Lucknow is.

Sanobar: The culture of Lucknow is an amalgamation of complete sophistication, warmth, manners (etiquette), courtesy and a fine taste in the standard of living. Many cultural traits of the city have become landmarks of *tehzeeb*. Lucknow even has to its credit the tag of being one of the happiest cities (as revealed in a survey done by electronics major LG in the year 2015) in India due to its irresistible *nazakat*, *nafasat* and *andaz*. A Lucknowite has the convenience and the easygoing lifestyle of a citydweller while being spared the pressures of life in a metro.

Shweta: You know what makes Lucknow, Lucknow?

The question is better left unanswered. Through words, one can touch the frame of Lucknow. But the soul of the city will still be untouched.

The soul can't be reached until one connects with the element.

The monuments, the bazaars, the food, the clothing, the people, the weather, the temples and the mosques...

On the tops of temple towers
And the tips of mosque minarets
Always there sways a flag of love
That spirit in the flag that flitters around

And spreads across the walls and clouds of Lucknow;
What sails and scales new heights
in the small city of Lucknow
is the tinge of India.

The moon shaded blue in the dark grey twinkling sky
The moon that turns orange in the low cloudy skies
The crescent of Eid and the curved one of Karwa Chauth
All moons of Lucknow rise to glow in love and worship.

All eyes of reverence that never fail
to catch a glance and dance to the single one in the sky

that adorns and decks it up
as the sole beauty of the dark skies.

Its variant shades and colours
reflect all shades and colours of Lucknow.
You never miss the one up in the dark blue
You shall never miss the ones who bow down too.

It could be just anything that joins us together. It could be every single little thing that makes our anecdotes. Those narratives conjoin to create a world of Lucknow.

So the tailor down the lane, or a *sabji-wala* with his *thela-gaadi*, or a barber who sits for the whole day with a chair and a mirror under the tree's shade, they all become a part of Lucknow and it's their presence that enlivens the place.

Sanobar: A lot of importance is given to dance, music, literature, Urdu poetry and drama here. Lucknow's cuisine, also known as Awadhi cuisine, has a unique *nawabi* style. Lucknow can be called a paradise for food lovers.

The city is extremely popular for *chikan* and *Lucknawi zardozi*, two kinds of stylish and delicate Indian embroidery. The export of these rich materials forms a significant part of the revenue to the city. There is a huge demand for both these handcrafted embroideries, not only in India but also in the overseas markets.

The other famous industry is the small-scale kite-making industry. Other famous products of Lucknow include its *ittars* and *kivam*. The markets of Lucknow are filled with handicrafts such as silver and gold foil work, bone carved products and pottery. A walk through the old and narrow bylanes of Gol Darwaza and Akbari Gate in Purana Lucknow unfolds many chapters of this epicentre of culture.

Lucknow boasts of being home to various tourist attractions and a glorious architectural history which has withstood the passage of time. Roomi Gate, Bada Imambada, Chhota Imambada, the Constantia, Tare Wali Kothi, Chattar Manzil, Dilkusha, Khursheed Manzil, Satkhanda, Shahi Baoli, Nadan Mahal and Banarsi Bagh are some of the well-known attractions.

Shweta:

कुछ शौक तुम्हारे कुछ शौक हमारे हैं
लखनऊ में यूँही गुज़रे ज़माने हैं

I know that Lucknow is expanding. Change is the need of the hour.

There was a time when there were unique nawabi sports and the Nawabs liked to spend the entire day in leisurely pastimes, the favourites being: kite flying, rooster fights and pigeon racing. Hunting was also one of the prestigious sports and was symbolic of royalty.

They also indulged in listening to *ghazals*, *bait-baazi*, and arranging *mushairas*.

In the past, if there have been the signatures of Mughals, Nawabs and British on this place, in the recent times, the governments, with their own flags and faces to propagate, have marked Lucknow with parks and memorials. But Lucknow has its own wisdom. Lucknow is away from the weariness, the fever and fret. And this is because Lucknow dwells somewhere in the middle; distanced from the glorious noise of other cities, noise that leaves them isolated, the noiseless Lucknow manages to continue its silent journey without drowning into oblivion. So Lucknow resides as that magical land that is lulled by some enigmatic air that makes us all monarchs at once and simultaneously.

We don't hurry
We rest and compete at the same time
We make plans over cups of tea
We work for hours over samosas
On rickshaws and tongas
We imagine conquering the world
And we do win.

The settled India is here.
This is that part of the country which is
innocently mature;
This is that part of India which is beautifully
pregnant with
ideas, designs and desires.

There is music in the alleys of Lucknow;
Kathak dances to the beats of tabla;
Shayari and ghazals float in marriages and offices both.
That's Lucknow.

We're faraway people
We live in reveries
Thoughts in our eyes
For the unfamiliar

And these thoughts are gigantic
To touch the skies
Or be grounded for the whole life.
We don't mind if that chance

Is a never-ending wait.
We don't mind if that wait makes and breaks
us, we're happy running after them
We're like the painting on Keats' Grecian urn.

Where beauty sits more in pursuit than in achievement, we are the earthen pot freshly made that never loses its earthy smell, unpretentious, never hard enough, soft and adaptable. We seldom change but whenever we do, we change with elan.

Sanobar: And before we move on to explore the unexplored and explain the inexplicable, we must not forget to mention the *paan* which is an exquisite end to the dining etiquette of Lucknow. This mouth freshener still holds its intrinsic characteristic, with the paan joints or *tamboli ki dukan* being the centre of social congregation even in modern Lucknow. The history of paan revolves around the Nawabs and so does its paraphernalia, including the *pandan*, *khasdan* and *peekdan*.

Let's move forward with the amazing story of this beautiful and charismatic city, as the stage is all set and the conversation is in full swing.

किस्सा पुराना है, अंदाज नया सा है,
गुफ्तगू करने को, ये ख्याल नया सा है।

Endnotes

Ek mulaqat: A meeting

tehzeeb: culture

nazakat, nafasat and *andaz: refined and exquisite*

sabji-wala: vegetable seller

thela-gaadi: wheelbarrow

ittars: perfumes

kivam: a tobacco product

tabla: a musical instrument; a pair of drums that are played with palms and fingers.

paan: beetle leaf

pandan, khasdan: used for serving paan

peekdan: for spitting paan

Chapter 1

Re-Creating Lucknow's Coming of Age: Remembering the Nawabs

Sanobar: Every place has a past and so does our beloved city of Lucknow. Let's start with the historical backdrop. What do you say?

Shweta: Yes, and in our very own *Lakhnawi* way—poetic, luxuriant, historical and lavish.

You know how I would float Lucknow, in what stream and in which colour. Your history would blend with my poetry, and we'll gift Lucknow the most amazing thought book by two women romantically lazying over Lucknow, when 'doing nothing' becomes the major work done. We love to get lost down memory lane, reflecting over all those years lived in Lucknow, when we grew up in bodies and intelligence, and the city grew simultaneously with each passing day, when we moved towards our future and the city kept creating its history.

And we don't want to die with our feelings for Lucknow buried within us. We would rather express our gratitude and love and would also want that Lucknow loves us till infinity.

Let's start our tour with a dive into the ocean of Lakhnawi history and search for some precious jewels to make a lovely beaded necklace of times gone by...

Sanobar: To begin with, the dynasty of the Nawab Wazirs was founded by a Persian adventurer, Muhammad Amin, who was appointed the Subahdar of Awadh by the Mughal emperor Muhammad Shah Rangeela in 1720, as a reward for helping put an end to the tyranny of the king-maker brothers, Abdullah and Husain Ali, the Saiyads of Barhi. He received the title *Sa'adat Khan, Burhanu-ul-Mulk* and, with the passage of time or may I say taking advantage of the disintegrating Mughal empire, made his province virtually independent, laying the foundations of a new kingdom.

Shweta: Alright. Then what happened after Sa'adat Khan's demise?

Sanobar: At the time of his death in 1739, he left behind a well-organized kingdom and, in spite of the loot and pillage of Nadir Shah, the mighty Afghan invader, in the same year, also a plentiful treasury to his successor, his nephew and son-in-law Safdar Jang. Safdar Jang died in 1756 and was succeeded by his son Shuja-ud-daulah, who was also given the hereditary appointment of Wazir by Shah Alam, the Mughal emperor, in 1760. The close connection between the kingdom of Awadh and the East India Company, which continued until the annexation of the country in 1856, also began during his reign.

Shuja-ud-daulah died in 1775 and was succeeded by his son Asaf-ud-daulah, who shifted the capital from Faizabad to Lucknow.

Shweta: But why did he do that?

Sanobar: That is a very important and relevant question. The women of the household were the prime reason. It so happened that the Nawab's mother, Bahu Begum, and his grandmother, Nawab Begum, were extremely rich women in their own right, besides being politically astute. There existed an overt influence of the begums in the affairs of the kingdom. The royal women were allowed to retain the treasure of the deceased king as private property, in addition to some extensive *jagirs* in various parts of Awadh, which gave them considerable influence over the king and his affairs. So, to move away from the domineering influence of the begums, the Nawab shifted his capital from Faizabad to Lucknow.

After the death of Asaf-ud-daulah, Wazir Ali was proclaimed Nawab with the consent of the Resident and the Governor-General. He, however, due to his vicious habits and not-so-legal claim to the throne, was soon deposed and replaced by Sa'adat Ali, a brother of Asaf-ud-daulah, who since 1776 had been living under British protection at Benaras.

Shweta: What paved the way for the Company's intrusion into the kingdom of Awadh?

Sanobar: Well, with the increasing power of the British, Sa'adat Ali was now required to sign a fresh treaty. The Company undertook the defense of the Nawab's territories, against both internal and external enemies, and for this purpose, was to maintain a constant force of several thousand men in Awadh through the terms of the infamous Subsidiary Alliance, which the Company used to exercise undue influence over the kingdoms in India. Furthermore, the greater part of the Nawab's force was disbanded. This paved the way for the Company's incursions into the kingdom of Awadh to the point of no return. The increase in the payment of annual revenues to the Company added to the woes of the kingdom.

Henceforward, British interference was directed towards the improvement of the internal administration.

Sa'adat Ali Khan died on July 11, 1814, and was succeeded by his second son, Ghazi ud-din Haider, who was a man of letters and possessed insight into subjects like philosophy and science. He was well-meaning but unfortunately was surrounded by unscrupulous courtiers.

Shweta: This situation throws light on how some rulers, though having good intentions, were often subjected to undue interference and intrigue.

Sanobar: Yes, that's true. Even big empires all over the world were not spared by their own traitors. Later, in 1819, at the insistence of the British government, Ghazi ud-din formally adopted the title of 'King of Awadh' and started the saga of the Nawabs being addressed as the Nawab Kings of Awadh. In 1827, Ghazi ud-din died and was succeeded by Nasir ud-din Haider, whose identity is controversial. According to some historians, he was neither the son nor a relative of Ghazi ud-din Haider.

He is mostly known for his promiscuous lifestyle and drinking habits. Even his wife, of Mughal lineage, avoided his company and preferred a life of retirement on a pension. The king's *wazirs*, Fazl Ali, Ram Dayal and Akbar Ali took advantage. They left no stone unturned in emptying the royal coffers. Lawlessness became the order of the day, with a sharp rise in nightly robberies, murders and local rebellions. Revenue collection fell and the kingdom was in utter chaos.

Even the reinstatement of Hakim Mehadi as wazir (who looked after the administration during the reign of Nasir ud din Haider) to reorganize the revenue administration did not make much difference. He faced a lot of opposition for his reforms as they adversely affected the interests of many nobles and chiefs. Nasir ud-din Haider died in July 1837, ending the period of debauchery, viciousness and impropriety.

Nasir ud Daula was proclaimed as the new king, with the title of Mohammad Ali Shah. Unfortunately, the king was an old man and was incapable of bringing in the requisite reforms in the administration with the kind of vigour that was the need of the hour. He did his best to rectify the problems left by his predecessor but in vain. Mohammad Ali died in 1842 and was succeeded by his second son, Amjad Ali Shah.

Shweta: I wish to phrase it in my poetic way.

Sanobar: Yes, please

Shweta:

तोहमतों के दौर चलते रहे
सल्तनतें बदलीं, हुकूमतों के नाम बदलते रहे;
लखनऊ के चहरे को उम्र-दर-उम्र बादशाहों ने खूब बदला,
और जो बदल बदल के खुद फ़ना होते चले
आसमान-ए-लखनऊ ने उन्हें अपनी रूह में जिंदा रखा।

Sanobar: बहुत खूब! The composition is apt for the story of our dear Awadh.

Shweta: Thanks. Then what happened?

Sanobar: Yes, coming back to the tale of the Nawabs. The new king, Amjad Ali Shah, was a well-educated man, more so in religious affairs. He was a devout Muslim and a generous man. To him is attributed the famous couplet, *'जिसको न दे मौला, उसको दे असफ-उद-दौला'*. He was succeeded by his son Wajid Ali Shah who, according to British historians, was not a great fit for the existing circumstances. However, a deep study of the circumstances reveals that much was not in the control of the king. The undue British interference hindered his administrative powers. Revenue collectors and land-holders clashed constantly. The *zamindars* became robbers and murderers on being deprived of their estates due to the annexation of the kingdom.

The reign of Wajid Ali Shah has been projected by British historians as one full of ambiguity and frivolousness due to his indulgence in dance, drama and poetry. All reports about the administration of the kingdom were based on the foregone conclusions of Col. Sleeman and General Outram. No argument from the king was heard, which throws light on the vicious intentions of the British government. Consequently, Lord Dalhousie annexed Awadh on the pretext of misgovernment. A draft treaty was prepared, which allowed the king and his successors to retain their title and dignity. They were allotted the palace in Lucknow with the parks at Bibiapur and Dilkusha, along with an allowance of 15 lakh per annum. The king refused to sign the treaty and General Outram took charge of the erstwhile kingdom of Awadh. After three days, the king departed for Calcutta on March 13, 1856. This occasion was marked by a lot of grief and remorse amongst his subjects, which speaks to his popularity even though he was labelled as a frivolous ruler.

दर-ओ-दीवार पे हसरत से नज़र करते हैं
खुश रहो अहल-ए-वतन हम तो सफर करते हैं

These lines were said by Wajid Ali Shah when he was dethroned and exiled to Matia Burj in Calcutta. Now there existed no royal court. The former king reached Kolkata two months later but was not permitted to go to England to meet the Crown. Soon, the revolt of 1857 took place, with strong support and leadership provided from Lucknow by Hazrat Mahal, the begum of the king who had been left behind. As a precautionary measure, the ex-king was arrested in June 1857 and detained as a state prisoner in Fort William until July 1859. He was then retired to Garden Reach, Calcutta, where he enjoyed his pension of 12 lakh a year, until his death in 1887.

Thus ends the tale of the Nawabs and the kings of Awadh.

Shweta: Interesting...

Sanobar: So how do you perceive it?

Shweta: I would say it like this:

Lucknow stands and so do the delightful sketches.
2021... Lucknow has crossed an ocean of time to be at this shoal.
The Mughals, the Nawabs and the British
constructed a beautifully brocaded city
sealing it further with their uniqueness.

Lucknow was in the making...
Not just the extrinsic scheme
But the intrinsic paradigm
far more flamboyant and intriguing.
This fabric was designed.

Every ruler old or new
Painted Lucknow of their own colour choice
A blend of Mughal, Nawabi, French, British intentions dots the city

So what now stands is a rare mix of contemporary and antique character.

Lucknow moves yet seems still as waters of the sea.
There's turbulence around but Lucknow absorbs it all
Like that earth that doesn't shake
even though there are plates moving under it.
This quality is distinct and Lakhnawi
It's ageless and it's not about bouncing back to life
Like a tortoise it lives…and sustains.
Powerful and positive in a very different way.

Someone got Lucknow as a reward
Someone inherited Lucknow
Someone looted Lucknow
Someone declared Lucknow their jaagir
Someone sold and
Someone purchased Lucknow.
And here Lucknow stands after passing through countless hands of kings and lords
as the city of love, history and literature
And holds a special place in the hearts of everyone
Belonging or not belonging to Lucknow.

Endnotes

Bahut khoob: (बहुत खूब) *Excellent*

Jaagir: estate; domain

Chapter 2

Re-Living the Revolt in Awadh and the Unforgettable Role of the Begums and Tawaifs

Shweta:

क्यूँ न इस ज़मीं और आसमां को अपना कहने का
दम भर लें हम,
जो अपना था क्यूँ न उसके लिए थोड़ा मर के जी लें हम,
रगों की लाल सियाही से अपने अज़ीज़ हिंदुस्तान को,
क्यूँ न आज रंग-ए-शहादत से बेफिक्र रंग दें हम।

With the background, it is clear that the stage was set and the Mutiny was inevitable. The 1857 War of Independence was magma held down forcibly by the British. Violence and injustice meted out to the Indians for several decades had reached the vent so that the heat, the rage boiled to the brink and soon, like molten lava of an active volcano, it erupted as the flood of mutiny.

We are about to churn one of the most burning subjects in the history of Lucknow.

Let's unravel the history of Awadh since the British annexed it.

Sanobar: As we know, the kingdom of Awadh was a princely state in northern India. With the decline and disintegration of the Mughal empire, local governors in the said kingdom grew autonomous. Awadh was annexed by the British in 1856.

Shweta: When India was not India, but British India, in Awadh there were two fronts: the East India Company versus Indian patriots. Throw some light on the siege of Lucknow as an important part of the Indian rebellion of 1857. Who were the main front-runners in the East India Company and who were the Indian patriots associated with the siege?

Sanobar: The siege of Lucknow lasted from May 30 to November 27, 1857. Brigadier-General Sir Henry Montgomery Lawrence, Brigadier John Inglis, Sir Henry Havelock, Sir James Outram, Sir Colin Campbell, and James George Smith Neill were the leaders of the British contingent. The commanders among the Indian patriots unit from Lucknow were Begum Hazrat Mahal, Birjis Qadra (the son of Nawab Wajid Ali Shah and Begum Hazrat Mahal, the sixth Nawab of Awadh from 1857 until 1858), Barkat Ahmad (a leading figure in the Battle of Chinhat, he was a highly trained British sepoy turned mutineer), and Ahmadullah Shah of Faizabad. In the 1857 rebellion, Peshwa Nana Sahib and Khan Bahadur Khan fought alongside Ahmadullah.

Shweta: Our anger was a natural consequence of all that was happening in and around Lucknow. We resented the annexation of the province. We hated the treatment meted out to our royals. Discontent grew. As it is, there was never an absolute belief in the government; to find them generous and wise was out of the question. Distribution of greased cartridges was insensitive and mindless. It was impossible to curb mutinies and impossible to calm people down.

Sanobar: Yes, but destiny takes its own course and the destiny of the nawabi kingdom at the moment was sealed. Lord Dalhousie was busy with his malicious policies and continued on the spree of annexing states. The evil intents of the Company and the Crown continued unleashing vengeance upon Indians. Awadh was annexed on February 13, 1856. The British policy of non-interference was not maintained and hence, annexation was greatly resented. Major General Sir James Outram was appointed Chief Commissioner and was later succeeded by Coverly Jackson. The new incumbent did not hesitate in granting undue favours to the British troops. These troops indulged in acts of lawlessness and violence in the kingdom, leading to an acutely tense atmosphere where the people were angry with the governance. Law and order was disrupted and the nobility distrusted their new masters. Soon, Colonel Henry Lawrence was appointed Commissioner and Agent to the Governor General in Awadh to handle the situation. Sir Henry Lawrence adopted certain reconciliatory policies to ease the strain. He, however, was aware that the subjects had lost faith in the government ever since the incident of the greased cartridges. After the annexation, the former dependents of the courts of Awadh were reduced to abject poverty; the armies were disbanded, the artists and craftsmen lost their income and patronage, as a result of which many of them resorted to a life of crime and dacoity.

The revolt of 1857 finally broke out on May 10 and 11. The mutineers reached Delhi from Meerut, proclaiming the restoration of the Mughal empire and declaring the Mughal emperor as the leader of the revolt.

The beautiful city of Lucknow was transformed into a vast garrison. The city looked like a fortress with the government gearing up for an expected uprising in the times to come.

Shweta: When India was burning and there was heat all around; when it was imperative to be free and there was nothing more pressing than that; when slogans of '*Angrez Murdabad*' were ringing down every street of India, how could Lucknow remain behind? The *takht* of *Angrezi Huqumat* was losing its stature. The episode of the greased cartridges had paved the way for an outbreak. Who knew that a great mutiny was around the corner?

When the British had declared themselves the masters of this nation, little did they realize to what extent sentiments can be suppressed and patience tested; little could they foresee that the Indian soldiers knew about the greased cartridges and were not ready to remove it by tearing it out with their teeth, and little did they grasp that Indians place a high value on religion, which they do not compromise with. And adding to the British arrogance, domination and attitude of supremacy was their habit of taking Indians for granted and using power ruthlessly.

So India responded with the revolt of 1857. And so did our ever-so-peaceful Lucknow.

Sanobar: Yes, we at Lucknow were the flag bearers of the first war of Independence from among the royals. In order to secure the position at Lucknow, the Commissioner ordered Muchee Bhawan or the Fish Palace (which was built by the early Nawabs) to be strengthened as the British stronghold. Perched by the river Gomti, the old building held control over the river and the stone bridge across it. It could be used as a refuge in the event of an uprising. The Residency (the headquarters of the Chief Commissioner) also lay close to the river Gomti, on the same bank as Muchee Bhawan. The strategically located forts helped the government keep a watch over the city and its people.

The series of attacks in Awadh were launched by the Indian patriots on May 30 with the rebellion of the infantry regiments. The leadership was provided by Hazrat Mahal, the begum of the ex-king, and the movement gradually spread to Azamgarh, Banaras, Allahabad and Kanpur, Sitapur, Faizabad and Sultanpur.

The royal Kaiserbagh palace was stripped and the treasures were seized from the royal family. It is reported that the British soldiers even pulled down the upholstery and curtains which were embedded with precious jewels. Once the seat of power, the Kaiserbagh palace was pillaged by the ruthless British armies, in response to the rebellion. Away from Awadh, the leadership was provided by warriors and patriots of the likes of Nana Sahib, Maulvi Ahmadullah Shah, Raja Jai Lal Singh and Maharani Laxmi Bai.

Shweta: Today we casually travel on the roads of Kaiserbagh square, and it keeps reminding me of the days of mutiny; that there were precious jewels, pearls and egg-sized emeralds, tonnes of gold kept at Kaiserbagh palace which were later transferred to be buried in the main building of the Residency. Nawabganj, the bird sanctuary, was once the destination towards which Sir Henry Lawrence led a march to confront the patriotic regiments approaching Lucknow. Chinhat, well-known for its porcelain pottery market, was overrun by the British and the patriots.

The busy and densely populated area of Alambagh, well-known for its Punjabi residents, shops and marketplace, *sabji mandi*, and connectivity to the airport by the Kanpur road scheme, was once a prime attraction with a palace, mosque and a beautiful garden. The Alambagh Palace was converted into a fort in November 1857 and was converted into a military post by the patriots. Then it came under the commissioner-ship of Sir Outram. Later, with the arrival of Sir Colin Campbell, it was taken over and treated as the military command centre for Lucknow.

Sanobar: Yes, it seems unreal. During Outram's time, there were attacks on the side of the river Gomti and armies advanced through the Chattar Manzil palace complex. The English advances were made to take charge of the Residency. During the crossfire that ensued, Sir Henry Lawrence was fatally injured and finally succumbed to his injuries.

The beloved king of the people of Awadh, Wajid Ali Shah, was imprisoned in Fort William, Calcutta. Indians were constantly complaining of being controlled by foreigners and losing their sovereignty. Meanwhile, the British, were utterly convinced of their racial superiority. Several battles were fought at various fronts in Lucknow which changed the destiny and the face of the once-fabled city.

Shweta: So the memorable siege of the Residency at Lucknow had now commenced.

Sanobar: The death of Henry Lawrence added to the woes of the British at the Residency. There was utter chaos and confusion and fear. Begum Hazrat Mahal, meanwhile, rose to take command over the situation. The assaults continued from both sides, leading to severe losses and casualties on both sides. Firing continued unceasingly through days and nights on certain occasions. Soon, ammunition supply arrived for the English and so did Havelock and Outram, thus strengthening the British position.

Shweta: Well, that means that arms, ammunition and military supplies were imported along the river banks and all preparations were secured for an out-and-out combat, with Outram determined to win the city against the patriots.

Sanobar: Absolutely. The assault began under Havelock and Outram, covering the areas of Kaiserbagh, Khas Bazaar and the vicinity. They were countered by the patriots under the stewardship of the Begum, who inflicted heavy losses upon the English forces. The carnage continued and the English forces advanced towards the Residency led by Colin Campbell. The British soon captured Chattar Manzil without having to face stiff resistance, which infused fresh vigour into the English forces.

Shweta: Lucknow was a cozy nest...thrown into the desert of revolt.

In the valley of ecstasy where
song and dance with sports and food
jam-packed the mood

And guftgu and kisse
Occupied dusks and peaceful nights
Where lazy mornings and drowsy tired afternoons

Were not filled with ambition or resolutions
As happy we were with our ever-so-small
Indulgences of chess, ludo or kites.

Leisure never lasts long
To believe it to be permanent and true
is a childhood fairytale
that breeds and draws on imaginings.

Our bliss was abruptly destroyed
As everywhere around there were no easy ambitions
There was this desire to rule, to kill,
To supersede.

And human gods need attendants and slaves
To satisfy their ego and fly their flags.
It was crucial to answer back.
We wanted our earth and sky

So here we were
On the plains of Oudh
Ready to combat
And claim everything that was ours.

Love, life and music
That was our constitution
And our whole composition.
We fought with our body and soul
We fought for our body and soul.

Sanobar: That proves that patriotism and poetry are inseparable and how history draws from words and words draw from history.

Shweta: Let's bring to life the leading lady who shone like a spark when Lucknow was rising.

Sanobar: I know who you are talking about—Begum Hazrat Mahal. Born Mohammadi Begum to Miyan Amber and Mehar Afza, she belonged to a simple household of Farrukhabad. A girl from humble origins rose to the position of a queen, earned for herself a place amongst men and forever remains resplendent in the annals of Indian history as the 'pride of women'.

Her father, Amber, was a slave, who was owned by one Ghulam 'Ali Khan', and Mehar Afza was Amber's mistress. Miyan Amber settled in Lucknow and worked as a *daroga* for a year before he passed away of tuberculosis. Mohammadi Begum lived with her relatives until she was brought to the king's court to become a member of the royal harem or the *Parikhana* as it was popularly known.

Shweta: 'Parikhana'! This word...ugh! (Talking to the term) Don't thou drag me to the fiery land of feminism as it becomes quite a task to undermine all the womanly anger that uncontrollably comes to surface when such ideas are known to me that they had a name and an existence. It transfers me from the subject under scrutiny to the question of power and hidden human desires.

Sanobar: Hmm... I understand what you mean. She entered the famous Parikhana in 1842. Mohammadi won the crown prince Wajid Ali Shah's heart with her innocence and talent of poetry, which left the prince wanting more. For a short time, the prince was completely besotted with Mohammadi Begum and even used to write poems for her. She is presented in portraits as a dark-skinned attractive woman.

In 1845, the heir apparent learned that Mahak Pari was pregnant.

Shweta: (startled) Mahak Pari, 'the fairy of fragrance'?

Sanobar: Yeah, she was. And she was given another name too.

Shweta: And what name this time?

Sanobar: Wajid Ali Shah immediately put Mahak Pari into *purdah* and gave her the title of Iftikhar un Nisa, which means 'dignified amongst women' as he appreciated her dignity that set her apart from the others who were so submissive. This child, who was also bestowed upon with the title of Mirza Birjis Qadr by the king, was soon catapulted into a world of intrigue and conspiracies, with her only faithful companion being the eunuch Mammoo Khan, who was also an informer to the young queen. Mammoo informed the Begum about the politics of Awadh and the discontent of the masses because the *angrez* were gaining foothold and had grown increasingly disrespectful.

Shweta: Eunuchs played a significant part in the royal families. In this case, Mammoo Khan acted as the informer and the link through which the Begum learned about the internal politics and ground details.

Sanobar: Yes, the role of eunuchs, or *khwaja saras* as they were popularly called, was very important in the courts of Awadh. The nawabi era was a golden period for eunuchs. Other than fulfilling the purpose of adding spark to the court, the skills of eunuchs were utilized from the beginning of the nawabi dynasty. Many of the eunuchs rose to positions of importance under the nawabs and kings of Awadh.

As providence would have it, the annexation of Awadh scandalized public opinion throughout India. The Begum, whom everyone thought was the closest to Jaan-e-Alam, was left behind. The plight and mental condition of Iftikhar un Nisa can be imagined when the king departed and she continued to live under the illusion of being the guardian of the kingdom. Very soon, she withdrew into seclusion, where she preferred to compose poems.

Shweta: Meanwhile, the larger design took shape as the First War of Independence started and the whole of India was resounding with the cries of freedom. By the order of the Chief Commissioner, the British progressively seized Lucknow's most beautiful palaces. Step by step, the beautiful buildings and palaces were stormed, looted and brutally evicted.

Sanobar: On September 6, the Moti Mahal palace, on Shanajaf Road as we know it today, was taken over, followed by an attack on the Mucchi Bhawan fortress. The first war started in Lucknow on Tuesday, June 30, 1857 at Ismailganj near Chinhat. The English forces were defeated and found refuge in the Residency. Out of the eight sons of Jaan-e-Alam, only Birjis Qadr could be declared as the heir apparent. Begum Hazrat Mahal, along with Birjis Qadr, arrived at the *Baradari* and the prince was proclaimed king with his mother by his side.

Shweta: 'Baradari'. Whenever this name is uttered, it creates a very strange contortion in my stomach. I can't explain this feeling but 'Baradari' makes me visualize my little self when I was hardly eight or nine years old. Probably it was a word I used to hear as an instruction to the *rickshaw wallahs* to reach different places: "भैया पहले बारादरी चलो फिर आगे का रास्ता बताते हैं..." This building creates an outlandish feeling as a witness to my growing years. It was always there, timeless, for marriages, for exhibitions. Some places do not have a timeline; they are as much there today as they were once in the past.

Sanobar: Yes, I think there is not a Lucknowite who does not know about Baradari or more specifically, the Safed Baradari. This ethereal building was built by Wajid Ali Shah and has 12 doors, as the name suggests. Coming back, the queen and her son proved to be immensely popular amongst the masses and the Begum became a great administrator, as is evident through her royal decrees.

The carnage and devastation of the glorious kingdom of Awadh was now, however, irreparable. By August 1857, two-thirds of the Bengal army had joined the rebellion and efforts were made to quicken the pace of the revolt, bringing within its fold the Nizam of Hyderabad and the Maharajas of Gwalior and Indore. Nana Sahib soon joined in, keeping the interest of the nation primary over his personal considerations and prejudices.

Hazrat Mahal and her allies prepared for an attack. Tunnels were dug and underground mines were set up for explosions and attacks. However, the British counterparts under Colonel Inglis were keeping track of their enemies and were prepared to take the Indians unaware. For some time, the allies were able to build some pressure on the English armies but this did not last for long. The weather gods and the weak artillery proved to be a drawback for the Indian armies.

Shweta: Hazrat Mahal displayed the iron will of a true sovereign and served deserving punishment to the traitors. Amidst the palace intrigue and conspiracies, she maintained the composure of a ruler undaunted in her decisions and deeds.

Sanobar: She did in fact give the impression of being the most suitable leader amongst the men of those times. She definitely deserves accolades for being benevolent towards her subjects irrespective of their background, attending to their pleas and devoting time to them. Eminent English and Indian historians like Ball, Basu, Sherar, Mir Zair, Russel, Sunder Lal, Zakaullah and others are eloquent on the military and administrative abilities of Hazrat Mahal. To her goes the credit of not only leading the revolt at Lucknow but also of defying the English with some success. She bravely defeated the enemy in many battles, and also successfully and elegantly eluded their hunting armies on defeat. These and many more were no mean achievements in the dire circumstances of those times.

Meanwhile, the revolt spread across the country. Indians were full of enthusiasm though unsupported by the majority of the royals who were betting on the British success. Finally, the British reinforcements reached Awadh under Outram and Havelock. The Begum was prepared to face the challenge. The brave woman participated actively in the battle to boost the morale of the soldiers and to avenge the humiliation Outram had hurled on the royal family. The fall of Alambagh proved to be a strategic victory for the British. The battle of June was won by the Indians; however, the victory was short-lived. As anticipated, the British soon acquired control over Dilkusha, La Martiniere and Bibiapur. One by one, the Begum's fortifications fell. She continued fighting even as her palace at Kaiserbagh was being stormed. Hazrat Mahal was the last leader to retreat when the Indian contingent was defeated in Lucknow on March 18, 1858. Finally, she had to escape to the Musa Bagh palace, where the final battle ensued on March 19, 1858. Despite all odds, the Begum reappeared on the battlefield riding an elephant. For five days and nights, the palace resisted the Howitzer attacks.

However, victory was now elusive and she had to flee. Hazrat Mahal was given refuge by the Raja of Bhitauli. She continued to lead the resistance from the fort but was never able to re-establish herself and her son in Lucknow. The city finally fell to the assault of the British. The balance turned in favour of the enemy and the Begum had to leave for Nepal, where she was almost confined by Raja Jung Bahadur, who was an ally of the British. The Begum started a new and very difficult life but refused to return to India after the assumption of direct power by the English queen. She died in Kathmandu in 1879.

Shweta: It was her sincerity of purpose that attracted over one and a half lakh rebel sepoys and native soldiers—an army numerically larger than those commanded by any other Indian leader elsewhere during the revolt.

Sanobar: Amazing indeed! This army consisted mainly of the people of Awadh and most of them were retained by the rajas, *jagirdars* and *talukdars* who were the vassals of the erstwhile kingdom and allies of Hazrat Mahal in the freedom struggle. Historians are also surprised to find that the revenues and taxes, which used to be paid to previous rulers of Awadh only after much harassment and bloodshed, were paid to Hazrat Mahal promptly by the same landholders.

Her sacrifices were honoured by the grateful nation by naming the erstwhile Victoria Park in Lucknow as Begum Hazrat Mahal Park in 1962 and the issuance of a stamp in her memory on May 10, 1984.

Shweta: When the country regularly remembers some select heroes of the freedom struggle, the high sacrifices of Begum Hazrat Mahal and her family hardly find space, although the entire family remained a staunch embodiment of Hindu-Muslim unity, especially during trying times.

Well, that was the Begum, the epitome of courage. Let's also remember the courtesans of Lucknow, who were no less and proved their undaunted chivalry and mental strength during the Indian Revolt.

They were the elite, the richest,
the writers, scholars and poets,
the rebels and the activists,
The women who could read and write.
They were the intelligent and most desired women;
They were the courtesans of Lucknow.
Those who turned the tables
And reversed the balance.
They weren't thrown into the so-called hell.
This was a hell that they chose above
the so-called heaven of society.
They had learned through experience that what
the world so belligerently and outrageously avowed
As the malicious grounds that bred nothing but
sin and the wrath of gods.
A place that was stamped as one that drained one
and all of their respectability
A place that harboured venereal diseases,
was actually a place where they could lead a life free of slavery.
Here they were not poor, disgraced, beaten wives
Here they were not the unpaid labourers

Here they were not at the receiving end of their
husbands' betrayal.
Here they were the queens and the princesses of
some kingdom
Where there were no patriarchal rules and kings
to rule them
Here they owned their beauty
Flaunted it
And here they prayed for the birth of a girl child
Celebrated it
Here they were never widows
Here they were not cleaning the dirt
Here they were not getting raped
They did not hide behind
the curtains of their houses
or behind the veils
Here they owned their bodies
Charged their prices
Here they charmed the world
with their so-called vices.

Sanobar: When we talk about the women of Awadh, we cannot but mention the courtesans of the kingdom. These courtesans occupied an important place in the history of the region. These infamous women made important contributions towards the development of culture and were brave soldiers, conspirators and messengers at the forefront and behind the scenes of the war of 1857.

Shweta: The *kothas* of the courtesans served as hideouts for the rebels and the wealth accumulated by them also provided financial support to the cause.

Sanobar: The tale of Azzezunbai is one such forgotten story of the courtesans of Awadh. She was no exception to the marginalization of the voices and roles of women. This was primarily because of the disproportionately bad reputation of these female entertainers. Such women artistes in the various kingdoms of India were referred to with great aversion and contempt. These infamous women were known as *tawaifs* in the north, *devdasis* in the south, *baijis* in Bengal and *naikins* in the area around Goa. These professional dancers and singers were dubbed as nautch girls during the British rule.

In his book *Nautch Girls of India: Dancers, Singers, Playmates*, Pran Nevile described how the tawaifs of north India enjoyed wealth, power, prestige, political access, and were considered authorities on culture. In Awadh, these women formed a part of the king's revenue and led a life of luxury under royal patronage. The courtesans provided training in tehzeeb, or etiquette, and 'the art of conversation' to the younger members of the royal family. They were symbols of status and sophistication and distinct from prostitutes. In her work *Lifestyle as Resistance: The Case of the Courtesans of Lucknow*, Veena Talwar Oldenburg has described how these women owned property and constituted the tax-paying group in society. After the revolt of 1857, these women were however deprived of all their wealth due to their participation and contribution in the uprising. The failure of the revolt and the consequent British rule sounded a death knell for the courtesans who were gradually reduced to penury.

These beautiful, educated and cultured women of yore, who adorned the courts and harems of the Nawabs and kings, have been aptly dealt with in many Hindi feature films, the most popular being *Umraojaan* made by the Lakhnawi director Muzaffar Ali, starring the ever-so-talented Rekha. This film represents the position of the tawaifs, their homes as centres of culture and etiquette besides dance and song, and places where many royals and nobles would find solace for their non-peaceful souls.

Shweta: Yes, who can forget the extraordinary role of Umrao Jaan as essayed by Rekha.

They garnered wealth
And used it
For purpose high and noble

Behind the shimmering hanging curtains
Of sea-shells and trinkets and beads
And threads of pink and green

Golden blue
The pricey chandeliers
And oil lamps

There was a burning desire
of an invincible warrior
That smoked away all fears

These stunning women
Were valiant and daring
Indifferent to what the sphere

Regarded them as
Their wisdom and chivalry
Made them focus on issues graver.

Endnotes

takht: throne

sabji mandi: vegetable market

kisse: anecdotes

daroga: inspector

rickshaw wallahs: rickshaw pullers

Bhaiya, pehle Baradari chalo phir aage ka raasta batate hain भैया पहले बारादरी चलो फिर आगे का रास्ता बताते हैं: *(A polite way of addressing someone) Reach Baradari first, then we'll let you know the route.*

rajas, jagirdars and talukdars: kings, vassals, landholder

kothas: brothel

Chapter 3

Painting Lucknow with Colours of Poetry, Dance and 'Ishq'

Shweta:

इस कदर इश्क में बर्बाद हुए हजारों दिल-ओ-जान
लखनऊ ने मुस्कुरा कर कहा चलो कुछ तो आबाद हुए हम

There seems no better way to refer to the *fizaa-e-ishq* of Lucknow than relating it to the poetry, music and dance of Lucknow.

Music and dance have always added more colour to the amazing feeling of love. It can be unarguably declared that where there's love, there's music. Lucknow is no exception. Here, in every gully, nukkad and mohalla, there blooms a love story and in every gully, nukkad and mohalla, rhythm and beats overflow.

To define a city through feelings, memories and abstract ideas seems too metaphysical and romantic. But more than physical realities, we have captured Lucknow through our camera lens of fond reminiscences, smells and desires.

Sanobar: Lucknow, where love breeds and prospers, is the haven of love.

For instance, the zoo and Kukrail Reserve Forest (the habitat of the ghariyal) are now less the children's picnic spots that they once used to be (though we still find families with their tiny ones frequenting these places on Sundays and public holidays) and more lovers' destinations.

Shweta: Here, Valentine's Day is a special occasion when shops, markets and malls are painted red, not so much with the colour as with the feeling. Florists, on sidewalks and on dividers, on the IT square, on the inner roads in Aligang, Gomtinagar or Mahanagar, in fact all over Lucknow, bask in the festivity. And so do the greeting card sellers.

Hidden passions reside here in hearts that know very well that the setting of their love story is exclusively and extraordinarily 'Lucknow'. Artists and poets and craftsmen, office-going or college-going, all harbour this heavenly feeling in their bosoms. And they are not afraid to take the dive, to experience the divinity, into the ocean of sudden outbursts, disappointments and sometimes even reaching the shores with the treasure of true love.

The city turns and angles where love breathes in eyes and hearts; here love is the most charming and the shyest one.

Love lingers around universities and colleges and then rushes towards the shade under the Ashoka trees, behind a veil in parks and under the smile of lips in library corners.

Sometimes boldly moving hand in hand on the streets of Hazratganj, or brazenly during late nights on bikes in Gomtinagar;

Sometimes too scared to face the world it hides behind the dressmaker's dummies in the Chowk bazaar;

Or walks down the banks of the river Gomti and on boats to some unknown horizon for that little while.

But there isn't a qualm that every throbbing heart harbours it; some express and win it; some preserve its memory and it lives as a tear in their eyes;

Here love comes with the downpour in August and sweeps the eyelashes; the shivering cold of January brings love in the mantles of mist and fog;

And flies high in the sky in different shades of kites on Makar Sankranti; smoke from the cups of tea, adventure, warmth and zeal;

Here love does not fear to break through the scorching noon of May and June; to smoothly settle down in moonlit nights in desperate hearts;

A peep inside, a step into and a breath of Lucknow, and you'll meet a magical world of poets and their poetry—a world of *dastans*, *ghazals* and *qasidahs*. Here, Urdu floats in *mizaaj*. Who would want to miss the poetic enchantment of *lafz* that flowered and flourished to its zenith on Lakhnawi *zameen* under the lavish patronage of the Awadh Nawabs.

Sanobar: Let's start with Akhtar.

Nawab Wajid Ali Shah, the last king of Awadh, was a poet and wrote under the pen name 'Akhtar'.

He preferred to write in a simple language to reach the common folk.

And though he was well versed in Persian and Urdu, he invented his own style by adding a tint of the local dialect, Awadhi. That is why he was labelled as a poet of the masses and must be credited for making 'popular literature' fashionable.

He was into everything related to art. If he wrote an autobiographical *Huzn-i-Akhtar*, then he also wrote a treatise on music and dance titled *Bani*.

One of my favourite compositions of Wajid Ali Shah 'Akhtar' is:

तुराब-ए-पा-ए-हसीनान-ए-लखनऊ है ये
ये ख़ाकसार है 'अख़्तर' को नक़्श-ए-पा कहिए

Shweta: Nawab Wajid Ali Shah kept his court rich with poets and opulent with poetry, theatre and the performing arts. Lucknow was embellished and embroidered with art. Patronage was essential and ceremonial, whether out of dire need or royal habit or just for the love of poetry and dance. Patronage blossomed, supporting all beautiful writers from Amanat to Ghalib.

Sanobar: Being a multifaceted man, Wajid Ali Shah evolved two distinct forms of Kathak: *Rahas*, the Persianized name for *Raasleela* (the dramatic form of theatre including acting, dancing and music), and *Raas* (a purely religious form).

Kathak moved out of temples and the Nawab added *rasa* and *bhava* to the dance, thus enriching it further.

Shweta: Lucknow is a beautiful handmade quilt with the most astounding and ravishing patchwork of distinct styles—sometimes elaborate designs of *rasa*, *rahas*, *raga* and *raginis*, and sometimes with simple yet striking patterns of *thumri*, *nazm* and *afsana*. And sometimes, it is so artistic that you would want to wear it as a cloak and dance to the *taal* and *thaap* of Kathak.

Even those who don't have any idea of this soulful, velvety culture will feel the vibes of this splendidly grand and aesthetically sensual city.

A culture of theatre and performing arts, of *jashn* and *mela*, of *mushaira*, of Kathak that moved out of the temples to the tawaif kothas with *mujra* and *nakhra*, which would soon be established as the most renowned and graceful dance form favoured by Hindi cinema and classical maestros alike: This is Lucknow.

Lucknow was the magnet that pulled musicians, dancers and poets to itself.

This land has its own charisma. It is a place of festivities and celebrations, of jashn and drama, of fairs, fairies, carnivals. One cannot afford to miss the extravaganza of Lucknow Mahotsava, a *maha utsav*, a grand festival, organized every year in the city. People of all religions participate with zeal and merriment from every locality in Lucknow.

Sanobar: There was a Parikhana in Lucknow, and a lineage of music and dance in the Lucknow Gharana. *Jogiya Jashn*, a spectacular mela, was a unique feature of Lucknow, in which Wajid Ali Shah dressed as a *yogi* and all the *pariyan* (fairies) surrounded him and danced as *jogans*. All Lucknow citizens were invited to participate irrespective of caste and creed.

Shweta: Fairies remind me of our childhood games: *Laalpari*, *Neelipari*, *Sonpari*; and of marvellous childhood stories as *pariyon ki kahaniyan* and *jalpari ke kisse*.

With rahas, jogiya jashn and dance dramas, one can imagine what magnificence and splendour Lucknow enjoyed and provided.

Love is a universal feeling. But when we read Urdu poetry that was at its zenith in Lucknow or listen to ghazals and *sher-o-shayari*, we realize that that special eloquence, that profound intensity, that pain in its rendition, is a "Lakhnawi" grandness which is peculiar to the city. So, to speak of love flourishing or dying in the alleys of Lucknow, is different and urgently essential.

In Lucknow, when a lover feels that love is gradually mounting and wants to express it poetically, they may say:

This day, nothing is more engaging to me than you. Tomorrow again I will find you within.

Years have passed and your permanence in my heart has established itself like an invincible fort.

It reminds me of the poetry of Khwaja Haider Ali Aatish, the great Urdu poet of Lucknow. One of Aatish's famous ghazals floats down in this manner:

कोई इश्क मिन मुझसा अफजून न निकला
कभी सामने होके मजनून न निकला
बड़ा शोर सुनते थे पहलू में दिल का
जो चीरा तो इक कतरा-ए-खून ना निकला...

Let's walk through those lanes where the gods of poetry lived, who wrote and recited and sang their compositions that melted into the earthy clouds of Lucknow like the ineffable feeling of petrichor.

The more you try to fill your lungs and stomach, the hunger is still not fed. As if the soul wants to devour the universe into itself but still will remain unsatisfied.

Sanobar: Of the many poets of Urdu literature who deserve accolades, one prominent name is that of Mir Baber Ali Anees. He grew up to be the Homer, Virgil and Valmiki of

Urdu poetry. He was also a celebrated composer and an iconic master of elegies of a bygone era. Born in 1802 in Faizabad in the kingdom of Awadh (now in Uttar Pradesh), he died in 1874 in Lucknow.

Mir Anees belonged to a fairly prosperous family of poets who had migrated to Faizabad from Delhi in search of cultural patronage. His grandfather, Mir Hasan, composed the monumental *masnavi 'Sehrul Bayan'*, which had immortalized his name. His father, Mir Mustahsan Khaleeq, was also a poet, famous for his humorous and satirical verses. The works of Mir Anees surpassed all his predecessors and contemporaries. He is still unrivalled in the realm of elegy (*marsia*), a form of poetry usually used during Muharram mourning. His father was his master but his deep attachment to his mother inspired the emotions evoked by him in his poetry. His own instinctive urge for learning and literature made him an accomplished poet. He was proficient in Arabic and Persian, was well versed in the Islamic scriptures and commanded fluency over the colloquial as well. The most distinctive feature of his works was the fluent use of Persian, Hindi, Arabic and Sanskrit words. This was the era when Lucknow became famous for its leading poets, Mirza Milamat Ali 'Dabeer' and Mir Baber Ali Anees. The historical spectacle of a recital by the two icons together took place in the famous Sibtainabad Imambara.

Besides being a master of marsia, Anees was also a specialist of *rubai*, the shortest complete poem in Urdu, containing only four lines. Mir Anees composed *salaams*, elegies, *nauhas* and quatrains. Muharram and Mir Anees have become synonymous among Urdu lovers of the Indian subcontinent. Mir Anees is a great teacher and inspiration for generations. Undoubtedly, Urdu derives much of its strength from his marsias. Mir Anees drew upon his vocabulary of Arabic, Persian, Urdu/Hindi/Awadhi in such good measure that he symbolizes the full spectrum of the cultural mosaic that Urdu has come to be. No Urdu poet from Ghalib onwards has lagged behind in showering eulogies on Mir Anees:

'किसी ने तेरी तरह से य अनीस, अरूस-इ-सुखं को संवारा नहीं'

Shweta: The city has had this ambiance about it that has produced shayars and poets even if they were artisans and ordinary workers, unlettered and poor.

It is a commonly known fact that the Lucknow school of poetry was an extension of the Delhi school of poetry. Poets migrated from Delhi to Lucknow and established Urdu poetry in the city. Sirajuddin Ali Khan-e Arzu (1689–1759), Sauda (1713–80), Mir Taqi Mir (1724–1810) and Mir Soz (1720–98) are some of the builders of the Lucknow school of poetry.

It is also well known that Lucknow poets focused more on style, embellishment and ornamentation. They made use of a very polished, stilted and elegant style of writing, and many styles of verses were invented by the common people of Lucknow, like *tukbandi*, *khayal* and *danda*.

Ghazal (an ode about the pain of loss or separation or even the beauty of love), marsia (elegies that are recited during Muharram in various *majalis* and *azadari* events), *masnavi*, *rekhti* (the colloquial verse in the dialect of women folk), *hazal* (humourous verse), *hajv* (satirical verse), *vasokht* (with eroticism as its theme) were some of the verse forms popular in Lucknow.

The houses of nobles, the residences of prostitutes, the sarais (inns) and fairs—all of these were the gathering places for poets.

Even the surrounding towns of Lucknow produced great poets. From Kakori, we have Mohsin Kakorvi and from Malihabad, we have Josh Malihabadi, who was also famously referred to as Shaair-e-Inquilaab for his work *Hussain aur Inquilaab*.

Poets titled 'Shaair-e-Inquilaab' and 'Lassan-ul-qaum' (a title given to Safi Lakhnawi) prospered in Lucknow. We had Ameer Meenai, the poet who wrote in Urdu as well as Persian and was close to Ghalib. We also had Mirza Hadi Ruswa, the great Urdu poet and writer who wrote the famous novel (later adapted into the movie) *Umrao Jaan Ada*. Then there was the learned poet Munavvar Lakhnavi, whose translation of the holy *Bhagwad Gita* as *Naseem e Irfaan*; translations of Kalidasa's *Kumarasambhava* and *Durga Saptshati*; and the Urdu translations of Gautam Buddha's *Dhampad yo sach raahare* are considered masterpieces.

Anwar Nadeem, Mohsin Zaidi, Majaz Lakhnawi, Brij Narayan Chakbast, Qaim Naqvi Jaysi, Nawab Baqar Ali Khan 'Ravish Lakhnavi', Surror Lucknowi, Shauq Lucknowi... the list is long.

Sanobar: This land has given birth to some Urdu shayars like Behzad Lakhnavi: *'मसरूर भी हों खुश भी हों लेकिन खुश नहीं"*; Mir Anees: *'गुनाह का बोझ जों गर्दन पे हम उठा के चले"*; Josh Malihabadi: *'लोग हम से रोज़ कहते हैं ये आदत छोड़िए"*, and many others.

Mir Muhammad Taqi Mir, an Urdu poet famously referred to as the god of poetry, was born in Agra but spent his later life in the court of Asaf ud-Daulah in Lucknow.

'उल्टी हो गईं सब तदबीरें कुछ न दवा ने काम किया
देखा इस बीमारी-ए-दिल ने आख़िर काम तमाम किया'

Shweta:

ऐसे देखें तो हजारों लाखों बातें हैं हमारी
ऐसे देखें तो सोचते रह जाएँ कि क्यूँ अलग सी हैं
दीवारें इश्क हमारी

Lucknow...
There's something in the name
Something too forlorn
Something left or missed...
Some agony...painful memories...
Some honesty that leaves you aching
Some innocence that leaves you pining for a soft
and abstract body
That you would want to hold but would not hold
For fear of fouling it with your own somewhat dark self.

Some soreness in my eyes and some soreness in yours
This is what comes with love
It doesn't matter whether one shares it explicitly or not
But the ache is there
And that's how Lucknow behaves.
It embraces the pain of all in a sweeter hold.

It is indeed true that here in Lucknow, *ishq* buds and blooms in bosoms as innocently as a flower, as rhythmically as music, as mysteriously as words that the soul suggests to the mind of the poet, and with the grandeur of a raja.

Endnotes

fizaa-e-ishq: atmosphere of love

nukkad: street corner

mohalla: neighbourhood/colony

dastans, qasidahs: story, elegiac or satiric poem

mizaaj: mood

lafz: word

zameen: earth

Laalpari, Neelipari, Sonpari: Red fairy, blue fairy, golden fairy

pariyon ki kahaniyan: fairy tales

jalpari ke kisse: stories of mermaids

Chapter 4

The Pulse of Lucknow: Food, Streets and Bazaars

Shweta:

कुछ लजीज सा कुछ अज़ीज़ सा
हर रंग बेहद करीब सा
लखनवी तड़कों की मिर्च सा
लखनऊ का हर स्वाद
दिल के पहले जुनून सा

The treats of Lucknow, the flavours of Lucknow. It's time to romance with the taste of Lucknow!

The fragrance of Lakhnawi *zaika* is the sprinkled *garam masala* on the *teekhi chaat* of the Indian multicultured setup.

Sanobar: It is always a pleasure to talk about the culinary delights of Lucknow, a city famed for its rich cuisine. Having been born and brought up and now settled in this fabled city, I have always had easy access to the much-talked-about, mouth-watering Lakhnawi food. The tradition of making melt-in-the-mouth *galawati kabab*, *dum biryani*, *kheer*, *chaat* and the never-ending list of mouth-watering delicacies goes back to the days of the Nawabs who were connoisseurs of food of all kinds. Most of my friends and classmates who have settled abroad or even in other places in India crave for all the delicacies and on every trip, ensure that they relish all that Lucknow has to offer, be it the famous Awadhi food, *khastas*, chaat, or the local food in various localities and *mohallas* of Lucknow. Most of the '*bonne bouche*' of this city has a story behind its origin. The most famous is the *galawati* or *galoti kababs* of the legendary Tundey Kababi located in the busy marketplace of Nakkhas and Aminabad. Legend says that these kababs were specially made for the ageing Nawab of Lucknow who had lost his teeth and found chewing food difficult.

Shweta: That's so interesting.

Sanobar: The royal kitchen was therefore commissioned to invent food that the Nawab would be able to eat without difficulty while still enjoying the finesse of the master chefs of the times. I still recall how any trip to Aminabad was incomplete without a kabab roll. This makes inevitable the mention of awadhi *paranthas*, which have an interesting anecdote related to Ghazi ud-din Haider. The king was fond of paranthas and his chef used to cook six pieces for him a day and put five seers of ghee into each of those paranthas, approximating 30 pounds of ghee a day. Phew!

Shweta: Imagine the calories! Today we would spend hours sweating in the gym trying to burn off those extra kilos!

Sanobar: Travelling through the bylanes of the market, I cannot but refer to the lipsmackingly scrumptious *kulcha nihari*, which I bet has no competition across the country. A trip to Lucknow without a serving of this delicacy is akin to sacrilege. A must-have during the month of Ramzan, it was cooked as a breakfast item for the Nawabs. The word 'nihari' originates from the Arabic word '*nahar*' meaning morning.

Nihari is a stew-based dish, made by slow cooking with meat and bone marrow. The rich Mughlai dish attained its final shape in the kitchens of the kingdom of Awadh. Traditionally, nihari was prepared overnight for six to eight hours in large pots for the working classes in the Mughal empire and was also used as a home remedy to treat common colds and fevers. Thankfully, I have learnt and acquired the skill to cook nihari at home and I'm proud of it. Savouring the piece-de-résistance in the Awadhi *dastarkhwan* is the layered bread known as kulcha, which is served with nihari. This bread is a crispy baked flatbread which is an inseparable partner to the nihari. The outstanding Awadhi tradition of '*dum pukht*' way of preparing food, where ingredients are sealed in *handis* and placed over a low fire, paved the way for the origin of the dum pukht biryani under the strict supervision of expert *bawarchis* of the nawabi kitchens.

Shweta: Share something more about biryani.

Sanobar: Biryani has been satiating the hunger of many for centuries but Awadhi biryani has its own story to tell. The word 'biryani' is derived from the Persian word '*birian*', which means "fried before cooking" and '*birinj*', the Persian word for rice. One legend takes biryani back to the days of Shah Jahan, when Mumtaz Mahal asked the royal chefs to prepare a balanced diet for the soldiers. Another story says that biryani was brought to India by Timur the Turko-Mongol invader. Over the centuries however, biryani acquired Indian flavours and the especially famous versions are the Hyderabadi and Lakhnawi biryanis.

There also seems to be no parallel to Lakhnawi chaat primarily comprising *pani ke batashe*, *aloo tikki* and *matar*. The word 'chaat' is derived from the Hindi word *chaatna* i.e. to lick, as in licking one's fingers while eating, originally being a street food consisting of lots of spices and sauces or chutney. I recall how we, as children, used to argue over pani batasha being referred to as *pani puri*, *puchhkas* and *gol gappas*. The most authentic local name is pani ke batashe, sold across streets and bylanes as a favourite of people of all ages. Even today, chaat is popular with anyone who visits Lucknow, with many joints selling delicious varieties all over the city.

Shweta: Chaat reminds me of tea. Let's have a tea break.

आइए आइए, चाय पियेंगे?

Wanna have a cup of tea?

एक कप चाय हो जाए...

Come let's have a cup of tea...

I want some tea...

My head is spinning. I wish I could get some tea...

Got up in the morning...time for tea

Flipping through newspaper pages...with tea

Raining...pakodas and tea

Bhule bisre geet on radio...where's the tea

Too much work...can't proceed without tea

Wish and desire for tea is almost always there. The most beloved beverage of all and nothing can beat it. Nothing can replace it. For some, it is as necessary as fuel is for cars.

And so we find chai *ka thela*, chai *ki dukaan* or posh, stylish and urbane cafes everywhere, thronged, and catering to the demand.

Art flourishes with every sip as tea boosts debates and contradictions. Fresh ideas overflow and the dreamy Lucknowites muse and write poetry over tea. Artists write scripts and painters draw a beautiful tale over tea.

There is something very ethnic and very local about this tea. It steals the heart away and the earthen pot aroma is the most heavenly experience. In that interval between sips, even the gods from the blue wish to taste this creamy, sweet concoction.

For those passionate tea-addicted mornings
Almost at every turn of the road
There is a tea shop waiting
To cater to the temptation
That kills all green teas

That breaks all weight-loss techniques
Because this is where we first binge
After every walk and run
And dip in excessive indulgences
Of chai bun and makkhan

No count no limit
It's just chai pe chai pe chai
People sit and talk and all happens with tea
Big decisions finalized over tea
An economical companion and the favourite mood booster

Even tea does not know how many
Depressed souls were ultimately lifted
Via its intake

Miss it if you can...
Door to the taste of heaven
If there was a drink up there that immortalized the gods
Then mortals on this earth too have their own
celebrated steaming hot thirst quencher

When you pick the tea-holding hot kulhar
The vapours that rise and the smell of clay
That lives in us...is Lucknow.

Lucknow's love for tea is world-renowned. Some prefer just tea while some drink it with bun *makkhan* (bun is a round-shaped flat-bottomed sweet bread sometimes containing fruits and nuts and a caramel topping), bread *pakoda* (another favourite fried snack available in restaurants and at street vendors, made from onions, potatoes, even spinach leaves, chilies, brinjal and other vegetables dipped in a spicy batter of gram flour) or samosa. What came down to India from Central Asia, and named after the shapes of pyramids as '*samsa*' and deriving from the Persian word '*sanbosag*' is our very Indian and Lakhnawi stuffed triangle samosa. Arab cookbooks of the 10th to 13th centuries refer to samosa as *sanbusak*, *sanbusaq* and *sanbusaj*. Served with green chilies and chutney, samosa is the most sought-after fried snack with a savoury filling of potatoes, onions, peas or lentils and even cashew nuts and raisins.. The *chaiwalas* hardly see a dip in their business because tea is needed by one and all. Be it a labourer fighting for the basic daily needs, an office-going worker meditating on routine tasks and reports, or a businessperson speculating over meetings and rises and dips in the stock markets. The love for tea seems insatiable.

Sanobar: True, but let's not forget the Awadhi desserts. The city has no dearth of sweet meals and boasts of a variety. Our favourite is the *makhan malai*. This is a sweet, fluffy and cloud-like dessert which disappears in the mouth in no time. The winter specialty is more than just a dish. It takes the epicure on a journey through the elaborate process that goes into the making of the dish. The culmination of milk, cream and an assortment of spices can all be tasted in each bite of makhan malai. Available only in winter, the dish has a mysterious bond with the season. Another popular sweet delicacy of Lucknow is phirni, which is a rice and milk pudding. This exclusive Awadhi delicacy is served in clay '*handis*' or little clay bowls of different shapes and sizes at the food joints serving authentic Awadhi cuisine, traditionally called *kaghazi*. The *kaghazi handis* were kept in the *dastatkhan* of the Nawabs of Awadh and used to be one of their favourite sweet dishes. The Nawabs of Lucknow preferred to have phirni in handis as it enhanced the aroma. *Zarda* or orange or yellow-coloured saffron rice is another must-have on the *dastarkhwan* of those in love with the food delicacies of the city. The name originated from an Urdu word '*zard*' which means yellow. Additional dried milk (*khoya*), nuts and raisins make it all the more tempting.

I clearly remember some of my relatives mixing the *pulao* (which is often used as a replacement word for biryani) and zarda and making a potpourri which they called *muttanjan*, but which always stood out to me as one of the weirdest combinations. However, the history of this exclusive Awadhi dish dates back to the Mughals. Variations were made to the dish where fried meat pieces known as *mutanjan* were added. It is said that this used to be the most favourite dish of the Mughal emperor Shah Jahan and was prepared on his request exclusively. Any gastronomic tour of our city is not complete without savouring *shahi tukda* or the 'royal morsel' if literally translated. This delicacy also originated in the Mughlai kitchens but in its present form, shahi tukda consists of bread slices which are fried (deep or shallow) till they are golden brown and then they are dipped in sugary syrup. Finally they are coated with *rabdi* (sweetened condensed milk). Saffron is also added for sweetness and aroma. One of the oldest and most famous desserts is the irresistible *malai gilori* or *malai paan*, which is a paan-shaped sweet filled with nuts.

Shweta: Where else to enjoy these mouth-watering delicacies? And yes, apart from food, it is clothes that are the major attraction of Lucknow. One has to mention the famous *chikan* work that is an inseparable attraction of Lucknow as far as apparel is concerned.

Chikankari is one of the most famous embroidery works of Lucknow. The word 'chikan' is derived from the Persian word '*chakeen*', meaning embroidery or designs. Lucknow has been able to preserve this 400-year-old art. Famous as 'shadow work', it is hand embroidery done very labouriously and aesthetically on cotton or chiffon fabric and it delicately decorates kurtas, sarees and other outfits. The most popular patterns of chikan work in Lucknow are *katao*, *murri*, *phanda*, *bakhia* and *jail kholna*. Lucknowites love to flaunt dresses in chikankari work and even Bollywood film stars don't shy away from confessing their love for this artistic embroidery.

Other works like *zari, zardozi, kamdani* and golden lace-weaving are also famous. Kamdani is a lighter work done with gold and silver thread, while zardozi is heavy work done with *salma-sitara*. 'Salma-sitara': this word has a very nostalgic feel. Though still very much in Lucknow now and always, I recall how markets with their narrow alleys echoed with the calls of the shop owners, "Come to our shop, madam, and we'll show the best piece available in the whole market, सलमा-सितारा वाला कपड़ा देख लीजिए." *Gota-kinari*, that is the gold lace and the silver lace-work fabrics, are also popular in the market.

Taking a stroll around the city, the two biggest markets of Lucknow, Hazratganj and Aminabad, are the most preferred and beloved choices. There are also many others like Kapoorthala market, Bhoothnath market and Sadar bazaar.

Rarely is anyone at Hazratganj only for shopping. Being the favoured terminus of coffee corners and bakeries, bookstores and cinema halls, Hazratganj stands out as *Shaan-e-Awadh*. As the evergreen heartthrob and the chocolate hero of one's life, or the chirpy, bubbly young girl whom you would want to woo for the rest of your life, Hazratganj is the most sought-after outing for Lucknowites.

In close competition is Saharaganj, which stands as a superimposed structure against timeless Hazratganj. We have been made to witness a mix of two different ages, centuries apart. Yet Hazratganj can never be robbed of its beauty and Saharaganj comes to become a part of it. With all the branded outlets and stores, beauty salons, ladies' tailors and ice-cream parlours, with 'Halwasiya' and 'Lovelane', the popular shopping places in Hazratganj; with Janpath hairclips, rings and bracelets, there is an ease, vintage style and antiquity that one maintains while 'ganjing'. Walking on the sidewalks, enjoying the seasons' drizzles, or beating the heat with sunglasses, scarfs and softy cones and orange or cola bars, or the wintry cold wind with jackets, shawls and sweaters on... 'ganjing' is indispensable and unstoppable.

Sanobar: Well said! Shaam-e-Awadh or the evening at Awadh to any Lucknowite is synonymous with an evening spent at the famous marketplace of Hazratganj with friends or family. The glitter of the market, the cascading lights of the street lamps, the vendors selling *rajnigandha gajras*, Moti Mahal *kulfi*, the coffee at Jabbar's, the stroll from Mayfair to Hazratganj Chauraha (now renamed the Atal Chauraha): all is familiar to anyone belonging to the generations before the new millennium. Hazratganj, the famed upmarket bazaar of Lucknow, has been a haven for shoppers and people on the lookout for some glamorous fun way before the coming of mall culture. Many governments in power gave this place a makeover and added to its old-world charm. However, the nostalgia attached to 'ganj' always makes us nostalgic for the years gone by. An aimless stroll in Hazratganj, generally known as 'ganjing' was one of the favourite pastimes of the young and the restless. But the place catered to all ages, interests, tastes and suited all pockets with a variety of shops, cinema halls, and restaurants. Hazratganj today is every inch the modern urban Indian neighbourhood, a colour-coordinated hub of cream and black. To any die-hard Lakhnawi, Hazratganj is the real showpiece of the city. Lying to the south of the river Gomti, this place has a great deal of history attached to it. During the 1857 war, a great deal of demolition was carried out by the British and many of the elegant bazaars and buildings in this area were destroyed. The place has been described as the property of Nawab Amjad Ali

Shah in the land revenue records. Abdul Halim Sharar, the great historian, writes, 'Towards the outside of east gate of Qaiserbagh were two high walls, beyond which lived Ali Naqi Khan and then Chini bazar, after this bazar was the gate of Hazratganj.'

After the takeover of the city by the British, a new but small market was established in Hazratganj to give it the look of a business centre. After more than two centuries, residents hold their memories of Hazratganj dear to their hearts. But the ganj was not what we see today. Before the uprising of 1857, it stretched from Kothi Noorbaksh (the present DM house) to Kothi Hayat Baksh (the present Governor house). The route was lined by many important buildings, including Taronwali Kothi (the modern-day SBI), Khursheed Manzil (now the La Martiniere College for Girls), Kankarwali Kothi, Begum Kothi, Kothi Inayat Sultan and a Shahi mosque which now houses the Divisional Railway Manager's office. Also included in Hazratganj were the Moti Mahal complex and the Shahnajaf Imambada. The market area was named after Nawab Amjad Ali Shah, the saintly ruler of Awadh who was popularly referred to as 'Hazrat'. The British arrival in Lucknow paved the way for the modernization and Anglicization of the market area with some new additions. St Joseph's Cathedral, an elegant Gothic structure with traditional church architecture, came up around 1868. This church was later demolished and a new cathedral as we see today came up on the same site in 1970–77. The famed Mayfair cinema, Kwality restaurant, the British Council library, Ram Advani Booksellers all stood majestically in the heart of the market area. Though no longer in use, the Mayfair building reminds many of the wonderful times spent there as it was the ultimate destination of high entertainment for the whole city. At the far end of the marketplace stood the old-time favourite Coffee House, which was the social hub for the elite. More than a restaurant, this place was host to great names like Pandit Nehru, Atal Bihari Vajpayee, Feroz Gandhi and Dr. Ram Manohar Lohiya, to name a few. Many business centres belonging to the era gradually were lost to time and renovation work done in the pre – and post-Independence period.

Shweta: Not to forget Aminabad, the other bazaar, surrounded by buildings adorned with nawabi architecture, where you move like a snail. And nobody minds as everyone dwelling in Lucknow knows the patience that's needed to walk down the lanes and alleys of Aminabad. Gully one, two and three, enticing lures for every girl and every woman with brocade and zari-embroidered *lehengas* and *sherwanis*, eye-catching salwaar kameez and designer sarees mounted on mannequins. You won't fail to buy colourful glass bangles from the bangle sellers as they shine more than the starry sky at night. So be it Gadbadjhala, Mohan market, Ganesh ganj, papad corner or aachaar point, here you would get a *khatta meetha pani* with bitter *jaljeera* in *pani ka batasha;* you would also find aloo and *chhole* with *khaste*; *kulfi* and *faaluda*, malai and dry fruits mixed *lassi*; *kachauris* and *chaat* and *jalebi*.

The land on which Aminabad market currently exists was initially in the possession of a son of the Mughal emperor Shah Alam II, Sikandar Shikoh. After Sikandar Shikoh's death, his wife sold it to Nawab Imdad Husain Khan Aminuddaulah, the minister of the fourth Nawab of Lucknow, Nawab Amjad Ali Shah. Aminuddaulah developed this irregular market site into a proper market zone with shops, concrete houses, gates on all four sides, rows to walk and a big park. After the mutiny of 1857, the market was taken away from the Nawabs and was in the custody of the British. Lt. Governor Sir J.D. Latouche renovated the market and the road that leads to Aminabad has been named after him.

An important feature of Aminabad is the park centrally located called the Aminuddaulah Park that became famous not just in Lucknow but nation-wide. The *Tiranga* was first hoisted by the freedom fighters at Aminuddaulah Park in 1928 during the struggle for independence. Mahatma Gandhi addressed the nation from this park during the Civil Disobedience Movement. Nehru, Bose and Vajpayee all spread the fire of patriotism through their words at this place. The congregation was brutally lathi charged by the British when they had gathered to listen to Jawaharlal Nehru. Now famous as the Jhandewala Park, for the flags of various Indian political parties fluttered here at one time. Often compared to the lively Chandni Chowk bazaar of New Delhi, the Aminabad market is a buzzing shopping zone, popular for the variety of colours, designs and prices in clothes, wedding materials, hosiery and chikan-embroidered material sold at affordable prices. Ornaments, jewellery, footwear, cosmetics, spices, dry fruits and books... one may think of anything and it is there in Aminabad.

There are other very old markets like Nakhas and Chowk that are noisy, vibrant and known for zardozi-embroidered garments, jewellery, food joints, and antique shops. If one wants to feel the pulse of Lucknow, see the true picture of Lucknow, with its sounds and tastes, then these markets are the right destinations. Here, one would find real Lakhnawi items like *ittra*, jewellery, accessories, lampshades, handicrafts, chikan-embroidered garments and traditional *nagra* footwear. With several shops squeezed in the narrow corridors, lanes and alleys, even encroaching onto the roads, the markets bustle with the noise of the crowd, as nothing deters buyers from indulging in a shopping splurge. Being one of the oldest markets in Lucknow, Chowk is the pride of Lucknow *shehar* in its own way. And it goes without saying that one can feed themselves with scrumptious kababs, biryanis and curries at Chowk.

All the markets of Lucknow are equally lavish eating zones with lip-smacking food which one cannot afford to miss or dare to escape. And all have that unique Awadhi ambiance that every resident of Lucknow is consciously or unconsciously aware of and that every traveller coming to Lucknow wants to experience.

Sanobar, what about a tea break?

Sanobar: (smiles) Sure. Not before I end with the famous and oft-quoted lines...

'लखनऊ हम पर फिदा और हम फिदा ए लखनऊ,
क्या है ताक़त आसमां की,हमसे छुड़ाए लखनऊ'

Endnotes

zaika: taste/delicious

handis: mud bowls

bawarchis: cooks

Bhule bisre geet: Radio program

सलमा-सितारा वाला कपड़ा देख लीजिए: "Please have a look at the cloth piece with salma-sitara work."

Chapter 5

Adab Aur Aadaab: Lakhnawi Mehman Nawaazi, Tehzeeb Aur Imaaratein

Shweta:

कुछ यहाँ की आब-ओ-हवा ने सिखाया
कुछ इमारतों ने सिखाया
सच है कि लखनवी अदब और आदाब
इस मिट्टी के हर ज़र्रे ने सिखाया

In Lucknow, there is no 'I', only 'we'.

So where's the need to be depressed and fall into an abyss of frustration and loneliness? Here the orchestra of 'loneliness' comes with a band of joy. So we are never alone.

That's the secret of any place that we love; where we love to stay; which belongs to us; which is ours.

This place becomes a person in our lives. An intimate, close and true confidante with whom we dwell in the valleys of warm mirth.

If only every new generation understood this close affinity which reconstructs the definition of culture and civilization over time and space.

Sanobar: Lucknow is a place famous for its culture and heritage. The past, particularly here in Lucknow, cannot be separated from the present. Distinguished by the picturesque title of 'The Garden City', Lucknow is situated at latitude 26° 52' N., and longitude 81° E. At first sight, it appears to be one of the most beautiful and strikingly 'Oriental' cities in India. Viewed from afar, the gilded domes and graceful *minars* rising above its many mosques, *imambaras*, temples, palaces and tombs convey an impression of fantastic splendour of a bygone era, in harmony with preconceived notions of what the capital of an Eastern potentate should be. William Howard Russel, the *London Times* correspondent visiting Lucknow in 1858–59, wrote, "Not Rome, not Athens, not Constantinople, not any city I have seen appears to me striking and beautiful as Lucknow."

The city has to its credit its own legendary history and several historical monuments and sites that attract people from across the world. The magnificent edifices standing proudly along the architectural skyline of the city are living examples of the Nawabi architectural ingenuity. Some of the famous monuments of this city are Bara Imamabara, Chhota Imambara, Rumi Gate, Chattar Manzil, Kothi Darshan Bilas and many more.

Shweta: I can completely understand what Russel must have felt when he declared Lucknow to be more beautiful than Rome, Athens and Constantinople. Even if I didn't know, then also just living in Lucknow with these monuments that loom large and speak a thousand stories, as if they have been standing as silent witnesses to all that has happened and is happening to the city, that otherworldly feeling would have been transferred to me. A beholder would always find this city to be a live museum with monuments sometimes making their presence felt and sometimes standing aloof to tell the tales of the times they have seen.

Eyes might have grown
Timeworn and weary
But this splendour is perpetual
And these edifices as sentinels guard with grey eyes
There is never an existence as naturally alive as them
And that is why
The oldest of the vast, huge trees
And these monuments
Strike an uncanny chord with Lucknowites
Immaterial is the calibration of precincts
As those who visit the city for the first time
Are no less affected...the only condition is
That you have to have a heart
To feel those heart beats.

And it depends on one's eyes how much one can look and create and save and fill up the crevices to make them stay and speak to us.

Sanobar: Enveloped in stories from the past, the most enthralling is the Bada Imambada, built by Nawab Asaf ud-daula, who was, to a great extent, instrumental in shaping Lucknow as a city of beautiful monuments. Popularly known as the Asafi Imambada, this edifice commands international importance in the world of heritage. Built in 1784, this monument was a technological achievement, having the largest arched hall in the world without any supporting beams or girders. On the top is the Bhool Bhulaiya, or the labyrinth, with intricate balconies and passages with 489 identical doorways. It is always advisable to visit the Bhool Bhulaiya with a trained guide.

Shweta: I remember how enticing the idea of visiting the Bhool Bhulaiya was when I was a kid. As the name suggests, it's a place where you will forget your route, get lost in the labyrinth and never arrive at the exit (if you are not accompanied by a tourist guide showing you the way out). As a child, I believed (and how strong was that belief!) that the Bhool Bhulaiya was a haunted tangle and some ghost resided in that maze that would gobble you up! It was eerie!

Sanobar: Another notable architectural feature of this Imambada is the contemporary adjoining lofty gate or the Roomi Darwaza, which cuts a unique profile with its large leafy ornamentation.

Another imambada in the vicinity is the Husainabad Imambada, popularly known as the Chota Imambada, built by Nawab Mohammad Ali Shah in 1838. This building is a splendid example of the architectural beauty of the city, especially because of its crystal lamps and chandeliers. Worth mentioning here is the tale of the tomb of King Amjad Ali Shah, located in upmarket Hazratganj. This imambada, which was on its road to death and decay, today serves as a live monument after mammoth efforts went towards the restoration of this imambada. Built by King Amjad Ali Shah and completed by his son King Wajid Ali Shah, this building was also witness to the war of 1857.

Standing tall by the side of the river Gomti is the Chattar Manzil, more famously known as the old CDRI building. This palace by the river, which stands abandoned, has many stories buried deep inside its bosom and once served as the royal abode of the rulers of Awadh. King Nasir ud-din Haider completed the Chattar Manzil complex and also constructed Darshan Vilas. Chattar Manzil is a great example of the Indo-French style of architecture in the city of the Nawabs. The majestic

Kothi Darshan Bilas formed a part of the Chattar Manzil complex and served as a residence for the king's begums. The building, which is being restored, is more popularly referred to as the Chaurukhi Kothi, or the 'house of four faces', as each side represents a facade of other popular buildings of Lucknow.

Shweta: The sun setting behind a monument with the Gomti flowing alongside grants stillness to that moment when seamless beauty can't be captured or spoken about. It can only be felt with every breath, sometimes with a smile and sometimes with a tear that waits in the eye but seldom falls. That tear has the power to turn the river water salty and thus stays within. Such are the dusks in Lucknow: smoky, dim and illusionary.

But then this paradigm gradually shifts to a morning when the blanket of exultant artifice is shed by the rising sun as it now colours the sky with bright orange and the twittering birds flying in the background or settling in the vaults do not let the world plunge into downheartedness because it's all about fascinating awakenings and fresh resolutions and journeys.

And thus continues the cycle of morn and eve in Lucknow.

Lucknow awakens to the sunrise
With the chimes of the clock tower
The impressive Turkish Gate welcomes the day
At early dawn the Hanuman Bridge and Parivartan Square
Resonate with the aarti of Hanuman temple
The silent banks of Gomti
Hold and nurture the city in their lap
Morning azaan unfolds the skies
As the city lazily gears up for the grind
The picture-perfect craft and architecture
Of the imambaras, tombs and vaults

Palace, quila and mosques
Moorish minarets, stylish kiosks
Decorate the city in diverse styles
The hot noons of Lucknow
Under the umbrella domes
Celebrate all festivities
And ceremonies
The foggy chilly winters
Cover these monuments
With a mantle of silvery icy dew
The Kaiserbagh Palace, the Residency,
The Constantia House or Satkhanda
Layered under the snowy veil
All speak silent but audible
Accounts that may or may not be recorded
Nevertheless these are the sagas and romances
Lucknow earthed, ground, carved and sculpted.

And what blend best with these quiet and serene, tall and magnificent prominences are Lakhnawi manners and mannerisms, etiquette and the warmth with which we greet a friend, a neighbour or even a stranger. Lakhnawi *tehzeeb* is famous. And it reverberates everywhere from conversations in kitchens, to drawing rooms, to opening the cab door or offering a seat at the dinner table. It has travelled across states, crossing borders and into popular culture through radio stations and films. Every Lucknowite is proud of belonging to this tehzeeb.

Sanobar: '*Atithi devo bhav*', or 'The guest is equivalent to God', is a concept adopted from the ancient Hindu text *Taitriya Upanishad*. *Atithi* literally means 'without date' and refers to someone who comes unannounced and has no fixed date of arrival and departure.

In the kingdom of Awadh, this concept of hospitality or *mehman nawazi* was taken to higher altitudes, which through time became the identity of this historic kingdom. The Quranic verse 59:9 highlights the importance of mehman nawazi, where the verse Surah Al Hashr says about guests,

> "But give them preference over themselves, even though they were in need of that. And whosoever is saved from his covetousness. Such are they who will be successful."

Guests enjoy a special status in Islam and treating a guest well is tied to the true faith of the believer. This kindness towards guests over oneself is an act of generosity recognized by the Almighty in almost all the religions of the world. The kingdom of Awadh gained a lot of prominence under the Nawabs for its mehman nawazi, which continues to this day in the modern era. The very famous '*pehle aap*' is known to all who are or have at any point been related to Lucknow and its adjoining areas. In Lakhnawi culture, hospitality is a sign of conviviality, cordiality and sociability. Even today, any visitor to the nawabi city is charmed by the gracefulness of behaviour which extends to Lucknawis of all religions and sects. *Tameez*, tehzeeb and mehman nawazi run through the heart and soul of the residents of Lucknow. One from this city does not become uneasy when guests arrive unannounced. Rrather, one welcomes them with the melodious couplet by the eminent poet Majeed Deobandi:

"अल्लाह मेरे रिज़्क़ की बरकत न चली जाए,
दो रोज़ से घर में कोई महमान नहीं है"

The poet is imploring to God and fears loss of earnings due to the absence of guests at his house. Such is the power of treating guests with all love and kindness to ensure one's own benefit and happiness. In consonance with the idea of *atithi devo bhava*, which in turn helps in boosting social bonds among the people, the legendary hospitality of Lucknow is steeped as a fabled edifice in the history of civilization. In modern-day Lucknow, where the past jostles with the present, Lucknowites retain the unique etiquette of mehman nawazi. It's the city, possibly the only city, where people routinely say *aap*, *janab*, *pehle aap*, etc.

Shweta: That's so true. And that's how we have grown up, learning the '*pehle aap*' culture and welcoming guests with all cordiality and regard.

Sanobar: To conclude with the words of Majid Deobandi:

'वो जिसको बुज़ुर्गों की रिवायत ना रहे याद,
उस शख्स की लोगों कोई पहचान नहीं है'

The poet hopes and recommends that younger generations must remember the traditions of the older generations to retain their identity and uniqueness.

Endnotes

Adab: respect

Aadaab: civility, salutations

Mehman Nawazi: hospitality

Tehzeeb: culture

Imaaratein: buildings, erections

Chapter 6

Stories of Lucknow: Reminiscences

Shweta:

ये जो कुछ भी याद है तुम्हें और हमें
जो बीता वक़्त ठहरा-सा तस्वीर हुआ है
चलो लखनऊ को जीते है फिर से
उन यादों के बक्सों को खोल देते हैं चलो।

Sanobar: As we reach the last chapter of our work, I felt the need to go on record with some of the narratives by die hard Lucknowites. These people who belong to Lucknow love the city and some of them even are proud residents of this historic city for almost five generations.

A discussion about Lucknow is incomplete without a word by Mr. Ravi Bhatt, eminent historian, an author and visting faculty at the University of Lucknow who specializes in the history and culture of Lucknow. Talking to him about how he sees the city through his eyes in today's world he travels into the 1960s, more specifically the year 1965.He talks about Ravindralaya auditorium situated in Charbagh. The hub of all theatrical activity, Ravindralay was famed for theatre performances and for entertainment of children through cartoon shows for a meagre 25 paise every Sunday. He reminisces how the city in simpler times was home to a couple of airconditioned movie theatres namely Mayfair, Basant and Odeon which today are not functional. He recalls his days at the University of Lucknow where mushairas and kavi sammelans were occasionally organized and when students used to be in awe of their teachers.He even quotes an incident when the poet Bekal Utsahi through his poetry was able to instill absolute silence amongst the boys who were getting restless. Mr. Bhatt stresses on the fact that the Tameez and Tehzeeb which was identifiable with Lucknow is gradually loosing stand in the blind rush behind the west. Bhatt Sahab even reflects upon the newspapers of the bygone times when there were limited number of publications like Pioneer and Swatantra Bharat, available in the market. They were known for the genuine information published and even the scribes enjoyed a very respectable position in the society.

A candid conversation with Mr. K.K Bali, a senior resident of Lucknow immediately sends him into nostalgic memories about his beloved city. He says that 'Lucknow of yore comes to me silently when I am alone. It always has a question on its lips which I want to avoid.'

He believes that Lucknow as city is fortunate that the condition of it's landmarks like Bada Imamabada, Sibtainabad, Shah Nazaf,Beligarad(Residency), La Martiniere College and many more have been considerably improved due to the efforts of enthusiastic young heritage lovers of Lucknow. The real damage which he visualizes is the damage done to the culture and Zubaan (language) of Lucknow.

He deliberates that 'Aazadi brought us so many good things like good educational institutions.newer job opportunites etc...' This not only resulted in the migration of a big chunk of local population to Pakistan but also led to immigration of Punjabis and Sindhi refugees who were forced to leave their places of birth. 'We also have the fair share of immigration from Eastern districts and other provinces who brought with them their own culture, language and cuisines. All these changes narrowed down the Lakhnawi nazakat and nafasat to certain areas and is now confined to a small number of a die hard few,' says Mr. Bali. He remembers those who have left an everlasting influence on him. His teacher, an Anglo Indian lady Mrs.Pepper admonishing him "बे अदब न फ़र्मबारदार लड़के, अपना क़ैएदा बस्ते से निकालिए। अपना इमला लिखिए" (You disobedient boy, take out the exercise book from your bag and write your assignment). His servant Panna Lal who acted like a guardian always complained that "आज भैया ने फिर नक़िस इमली की चटनी खाई थी स्कूल में'. He still remembers how a feeling of superiority overwhelmed him while riding on the Ekka on his father's lap which was more joyous than a ride in the Mercedes.

There was a gentleman whom he always addressed Nawab Sahib. He lived in the cantonment area. He was an Urdu teacher of British soldiers in his working days. His dress sense was unique. His Sherwani, payjama, cap and umbrella always had same colour. On certain days it was all parrot green and while on the other it was all white or all yellow. He spoke chaste Urdu and had beautiful Shers for all the occasions.

'At the fag end of my life these memories and faces roll around me like a film and always question me where have you misplaced the Lucknow of your childhood?' ponders Mr. Bali as he gradually wanders in to his world of memories from the past.

Next I was able to get the views of Dr. Amitabh Arya, Additional Professor,Department of Nuclear Medicine, Sanjay

Gandhi Post Graduate Institute of Medical Sciences who besides being a medical professional is also a quintessential Lucknawi.Dr. Arya often gets passionate about his love for Lucknow and hopes to contribute towards the preservation of the city's culture in some way or the other.He recalls studying from class 3 to 11 at Colvin Taluqadars College which enjoyed being an educational institution of repute and it was a matter of great pride to a part of this elite school.

Lovingly talking about his father Lt.Col. R.A.Arya, VSM who was in the Territorial Army & an IRTS officer, he remembers how he would take the family out to see Taziya procession in Chowk, during Muhharum. He would take them to church during Christmas to listen to the carols & see the lovely tabeleau of Jesus Christ, to see the various Durga Pooja pandals during Durga Pooja and in Dussehra to see Rawan dehan in the famous Sadar Bazar of Lucknow.

He strongly feels that "This is what makes Lucknow, the epitome of Ganga Jamuni culture, a fusion of Hindu Muslim brotherhood, a city known for the Awadhi Cuisine, the language of respect & wit" Lucknow being the storm centre of the first War of Indian Independence on the the one hand and a city of all kinds of refineries on the other.

He further recalls how his father would tell them that even the rickshaw wallah spoke the finest of the language asking the ladies "बड़ीबी आप कहाँ जायेंगी"।

The people have still somehow protected that culture of mutual respect for other religions,and have love and affection for their neighbours though the city is growing at a rapid pace in different parts of the city opines Dr. Arya. He hopes that the beautiful city of Lucknow continues to hold it's old world charm forever.

Every city is recognised by its legacy and not its present, is the opinion of the renowned historian Mr. Roshan Taqui. Sharing an anecdote he tells me that 'Lucknow is one of the important cities of the world which is recognised as the last integrated culture. Being a lucknowite is a reward in anticipation when you are identified to be. About 30 years ago one of my friend's was in Glasgow, a city near London. He had been waiting for the elevator to reach 6th floor of that building where he was staying. An old man joined him in waiting. After some time the elevator reached ground floor, the door opened. Seeing a foreigner nearby that old man offered him to enter the elevator but my friend said, "*No Sir, after you.*" Both entered the elevator one by one. That old Briton asked him as the doors of the elevator closed, "Are you from India, from Lucknow?", "Yes", said my friend, "but how did you come to know?" He smiled and replied, "Your gesture of courtesy and saying after you". And then he shared that his grandfather was an officer in British India and was very fond of Lucknow, so the reason why he was aware of the 'Pahle Aap' culture. The third phase which started after Independence has seen a sharp decline in values – the courtesy, affection and sophistication reflects Mr. Taqui. The essential Luchnawi spirit of frivolity and leisure has gone. The world renowned culinary art, handicraft have lost their finesse. Urdu, the sweet language of Lucknow is now a stranger. He recalls that there was the last public Mushaira in Rifah e Aam club's lawn in 1967. Tallking about present Lucknow he opines that the biggest achievement of this phase of Lucknow is that 'Adab and Aadaab' (Tehzeeb) have vanished and signature buildings (cultural heritage) are at stake. He admits that today it is emphasized that Change is the rule of nature which is true, but it is happening at a rapidly damaging speed so much so that – 'Yeh mere koocha-o-bazaar samajhte nahin meri zabaan, Apne ghar men kabhi mehmaan na hua tha so hua'

In conversation with Mr. S.A.T.Rizvi, a retired bureaucrat who is also a resident of Lucknow happens to be my last oral record.He believes that trying to express one's feeling as a Lucknowite is a tall order which involves an insightful capacity to reminisce what Lucknow once was.

'A Lucknowite of yore used to be a liberal, frank and honest fellow who derived pleasure from the awfully rich and a medley of cultural traditions which became an inalienable part of Lucknawi lifestyles during the rule of the Nawabs of Oudh. This has had a lasting effect in terms of social peace and, what is more, in establishing societal harmony overall. A typical Lucknowite even now exudes peace and harmony in his thinking and in all that he does. Making of distinctions based on class and creed and discrimination of whatever kind is as yet foreign to his way of life. This great historic city with Residency as an important relic of the not so distant past continues to remind the Lucknowites of the unequal fight bravely fought by Begum Hazrat Mahal, against the cunning and the better equipped British.'

The city of Imambarahs, with the famous Aasafi and the Chota Imambara together with the no less famous Hanuman temple and the Imambargah built by Raja Jhaoo Lal, among several others, is a symbol of mutual respect and consideration between communities in turn resulting from deeds spontaneously and performed by different religious and social groups led by the Rulers of Oudh. Lucknow is thus a unique city the face of which has not been smeared so far by big sectarian fights, attempts made in recent times by powerful groups to foment trouble, notwithstanding.

All of this, namely the historic buildings marked by a near total absence of religious and sectarian discord at any level combined with the spirit of camaraderie between communities which intensified during the mutiny to drive out the British has shaped the Lucknowite character and at another level, by the rulers of Oudh reaching out to the public at large, without distinction and discrimination, on festive occasions as well as on others such as during the course of construction of Asafi Imambargah when drought stricken poor as well as the not so poor were engaged for a kind of show of work and paid wages to ward off difficult times too has imparted a deep sense of belonging to the Lucknowites in general.

Moving on, the language, being the vehicle of cultural evolution, too played a very significant role in inculcating a spirit of mutual understanding in the minds of men and women all over. That language was Urdu which still rules as the Hindustani language of cinema, in theatre, and in media and in public speaking and now more often written in devnagri script. Late Firaq Gorakhpuri and Ram Prakash Kapoor and many others were inclined to regard Urdu as the equivalent of a whole Culture equated by them to civilisation in its entirety. Late Mr. Kapoor once wrote "Don't compose a requiem for Urdu yet and that is because some people if not all still spoke Urdu." In short, aided and abetted by the extensive and intimate use of Urdu language, the all pervading social environment has succeeded in giving shape to abiding qualities of head and heart that define a contemporary Lucknowite. Thus, the not so frequently used terms such as Aap, Janab, pahlay aap, tashreef laen, tunday ka kabab, Prakash ki Qulfi, Dastarkhwan, Chappan bhog, et all too define a Lucknowite at a mundane level. A typical Lucknowite not so well informed in times present is still found struggling to recite something from the great poet Meer Taqi meer and the threnodists Meer Anees and Mirza Dabeer – the three among the immortals of Urdu literature.

Shweta: As we reach the end of the book, it is not the end of talk on Lucknow. So much has been left unsaid, so much uncovered. But then that is understandable. This book offers a glimpse of that world which we call "Lucknow". And no matter how much we talk we still cannot cover the story of every lane, every square, event and person. And still Lucknow is shaping up. I know that changes are subtle; what is there today, won't be in future. My purpose is to preserve that slice of Lucknow which lives in me.

The city that has been known for its thinking minds and distinct seasons, Lucknow, is that place where the old co-exists with the new; old cinema halls blend with the new PVRs; where the old parks shake hands with the new ones; markets amalgamate with malls and multiplexes; *sabji mandis* co-exist with supermarkets; where longstanding Sadar, Chowk, Hussainganj, Udaiganj, Burlington square are as happening as the forthcoming extension and posh areas;

I looked up at the sky from my terrace and saw kites. A train of thoughts and childhood pictures rushed through my mind. I recollected the terraces of our houses that were joined so closely that the neighbourhood boys jumped from one to the other as they hurried to catch the kites that tossed and flung in the air. Those were the days when there were as many paper kites in the sky as birds. The green and blue shining marbles, the parrot that was more than a pet to the kids' gang, TV antennas that were to be fixed all the time, electricity that went so very often that we fervently prayed to gods to have it back to watch the Sunday movie at five.

Lucknow has brought newer perceptions and dimensions to my being. Childhood aroma merges with the youth and adult age experiential understanding of art, culture, tradition and so much so that, quite weird it may sound, but staying in Lucknow still pains me with nostalgia, a feeling that is associated with distance and separation. But staying here and yet being gripped with the pain of that place, fills me with utmost surprise.

Just as thousands of colours paint the sky in different shades, chandeliers with hundreds of lamps light it up, and millions of celestial spheres illuminate the night heavens, Lucknow sparkles thousand tints of hues and lights in the lives and hearts of those who have lived here or have ever been a part of this place. I would like to conclude with these words:

कभी वक्त मिले तो आना लखनऊ
तुम्हारी किस्मत में हुआ तो मिलेगा लखनऊ
मिल भी गया तो बात पूरी कहाँ हुई
मिलके जो गर ठहर गया ज़हन में
तो समझ लेना कि है यही वो शहर-ए-लखनऊ

References and Sites Visited

1. Sharar, Abdul Halim. *Gujishta Lucknow*. Bhuvan Vani Trust, 1990.
2. Singh, Malvika. *Lucknow: A City between Cultures*. Academic Foundation, 2001.
3. Sleeman, W.H. *A Journey Through The Kingdom of Oudh 1849-1850*. Asian Educational Services, Volume 1, 2. 2006.
4. Naqvi, Dr. Allama Syed Zamir Akhter. *The Study of Eligies of Mir Anees*. Mohsina Memorial Foundation, 2004
5. Mourad, Kenize. *In the City of Gold and Silver-the Story of Begum Hazrat Mahal*. Full Circle Publishing, 2013
6. Bhatt, Ravi. *The Life and Times of the Nawabs of Lucknow*. Rupa Publications, Lucknow. 2006
7. Jones, Llewellyn Rosie. *A Very Ingenious Man*. Oxford University Press, 1992.
8. Sharar, Abdul Halim. *Lucknow: The Last Phase of an Oriental Culture*. Edited and translated from Urdu by E. S. Harcourt and Fakhir Hussain. Oxford University Press, 1994.
9. Jones, Llewellyn Rosie. *The Last King of India Wajid Ali Shah*. Random House India, 2014.

10. Hussain, Mirza Jafar. *The Classic Cuisine of Lucknow a Food Memoir*. Sterling Publisher Private Limited, 2016.

11. Mahmud, Aslam. *Awadh Symphony, Notes on a Cultural Interlude*. Rupa Publications India Private Limited, 2017.

12. Hay, Sidney. *Historic Lucknow*. Asian Educational Services, 2001.

13. Tripathi, Amish. *The Times of India*. March 24, 2016. "King of the Arts". March 25, 2016, 9:59 PM IST, in TOI Edit Page, Edit Page, India, TOI.

14. Talwar, Oldenberg Veena. *Writings on Lucknow: Shaam e Avadh*. Penguin Books, 2007.

15. Taqui, Roshan. *Lucknow 1857: The Two Wars at Lucknow-the Dusk of an Era*. New Royal Book Company, 2001.

16. Akhtar, Wajid Ali Shah. *Pari Khana*. Kitab Ghar, 1965.

17. Azmat, Tahera. *'Begum Hazrat Mahal' in Women Mentors of Men*. Siddhartha Publications, 1970.

18. Wilburforce, Bird Robert. *The Spoilation of Oudh(1857)*. Nassau Steam Press.

19. Inglis Lady Julia.*The Seige of Lucknow: A Diary*. Createspace Independent Publication, 2013.

20. Graff, Violette. *Lucknow: Memories of a City*. Oxford University Press, 1999.

21. Raza, Sikander. *Wajid Ali Shah and Monuments of Awadh*. Hindustan Printing Press, 1974.

22. Naheed, Nusrat. *Jaan e Alam aur Mahek Pari*. Library Helpage Society, 2005.

23. Aminabad – Lucknow: Get the Detail of Aminabad on Times of India Travel accessed on 07th May, 2020. (travel/lucknow/aminabad/amp_poishow/47642515.cms)

24. Syed M. Rizwan, "The Criss-Cross Lucknowi Life", *Lucknow Observer*, May 5, 2015, accessed on 15th October, 2021. (lucknowobserver.com/amin).

25. "Aminabad, Lucknow", *Wikipedia*, accessed on 14th October, 2021. (en.wikipedia.org/wiki/Aminabad, Lucknow).

26. Akanksha Singh, "An Ode to Munavvar Lakhnavi, Famous Urdu Poet from Lucknow who Named Himself After the City", *Knocksense*, March 16, 2020, accessed on 10th October, 2021. (www.knocksense.com/lucknow/an-ode-to-munavvar-lakhnavi-the-urdu-poet-translator-who-added-made-lucknow).

27. "History of Lucknow", *Awadh Nawab*, accessed on 12th June, 2021. (sites.google.com/site/awadhnawabs/home/history-of-lucknow).

28. R.V. Smith, "How Wajid Ali Shah Lives On", *The Hindu*, December 2, 2019, accessed on 13th September, 2021. (www.thehindu.com/society/history-and-culture/how-wajid-ali-shah-lives-on/article30139222.ece).

29. "Lucknow Nawabi Glory", *shubhyatra.com*, accessed on 7th May, 2021. (www.shubhyatra.com/uttar-pradesh/nawabisplendor.html).

30. "Lucknow", *Wikipedia*, accessed on 5th May, 2021. (en.wikipedia.org/wiki/Lucknow).

31. "The Notable Shayars of Lucknow", *Lucknow Pulse*, October 15, 2015, accessed on 14th October, 2021. (lucknowpulse.com/the-notable-shayars-of-lucknow/)

32. Manu S. Pillai, "The Story of Wajid Ali Shah from Riches to Rags", *Mint Lounge*, September 16, 2017, accessed on 18th July, 2021. (www.livemint.com/Leisure/QHhVHqpy4HnPWouVFmFC1H/The-story-of-Wajid-Ali-Shah-from-riches-to-rags.html).

33. Mohd Faisal Fareed, "Unlettered Urdu Poets of Lucknow", *Two Circles.net*, April 12, 2011, accessed on 16th August, 2021. (twocircles.net/2011apr12/unlettered_urdu_poets_lucknow.html).

34. "Uteratuiis Uie Nawabi period witnessed great progress of Urdu Literature in its various forms. The traditions of the Lucknow" accessed on 15th October, 2021. (dokumen.tips/documents/uteratuiis-1pdfuteratuiis-uie-nawabi-period-witnessed -great-progress-of-urdu.html)

35. "Wajid Ali Shah", *Wikipedia*, accessed on 16th October, 2021. (en.wikipedia.org/wiki/Wajid_Ali_Shah).

Author Bio

Dr. Sanobar Haider

Dr. Sanobar Haider is an avid Lucknowite with a keen interest in teaching and learning History. Having a doctorate in History, the author has scripted many research papers and articles published in various national and international journals of repute. Having excelled in academics at all levels, she has to her credit several academic accomplishments. Presently working as an assistant professor and head of the Department of History at Maharaja Bijli Pasi Government Postgraduate College, Lucknow. She has been rewarded with various distinctions by different organisations for her outstanding work in the field of academics.

She is the founder-member and president of Avadh Girls Degree College Alumnae Association, Lucknow. The author has also been appointed as a member of the **National Archives Grants Committee**, New Delhi, and is associated as a mentor with the Uttar Pradesh Government's **'Abhyuday Yojna'** for civil services aspirants. She is a member of the Editorial Advisory Board of the Global Girmit Institute Indenture Papers and is a gold medalist in law. She has authored two books, ***Law and Justice in the United Provinces 1837-1937*** and ***Sibtainabad-Through the Lens of Time***.

The author has also had keen leanings towards doing research related to the history and culture of Awadh. The majestic monuments of Lucknow and the rich heritage of this medieval kingdom withholds a treasure trove of information and a legacy that needs protection and care.

This book is an expression of her love and fascination with the fabled city of Lucknow.

Shweta Mishra "shawryaa"

Dr. Shweta Mishra is an Assistant Professor in English and presently teaches at MBP Government Postgraduate College, Lucknow (Uttar Pradesh), India. A gold medalist in M.A. English, Lucknow University, she has authored several research papers that have been published in various reputed journals. Creative writing is what she passionately loves to do. Her notable works include ***What is a Woman: This is Trash. Leave it***, published by **Authorspress, New Delhi**, in 2016, and ***Image of Girlhood in the Fiction of African-American Women Writers: Paule Marshall, Anne Moody, Maya Angelou, Toni Morrison, Alice Walker, Ntozake Shange*** published by **Prestige Books International**, **New Delhi**, in 2011. Her collection of poems, ***The Most Orange***, has been published in 2018, by **Authorspress, New Delhi**. Her latest book, ***A Smothering Selfless Epitome: Sita***, has been published in July 2020, through **Kindle Direct Publishing**.

Her poems have been published in ***Kavya Bharati and Muse India.*** Internationally, she contributes her poems in the newsletter of the **Australasian Center for Human Rights and Health (ACHRH), Melbourne, Australia**. She has also presented her poems in the U.S. based online platform "**Bauchhaar**". She is also on the podcast – anchor.fm/shweta-mishra9.

www.ingramcontent.com/pod-product-compliance
Ingram Content Group UK Ltd.
Pitfield, Milton Keynes, MK11 3LW, UK
UKHW041820200726
13854UKWH00001BA/136

9 798885 036139